"This is one of the most extraordinary books I have read in recent times—a brave, compassionate, and astonishingly humane treatment of the challenges that face those of us who lead businesses. Taylor approaches and ultimately answers one of the oldest questions in business—where does the job of leader begin and end?—and crafts from it a positive view of the future where CEOs are freed to do the work that only they can do. Through his stories, told with good humor and lucid accuracy, we learn that we are not alone in facing the challenges in the C-Suite. We all are doing too much that isn't ours to do, and *A CEO Only Does Three Things* shows us how to fix that problem for ourselves and our teams."

—PETER BALASARIA, CEO, POWERLINE
HARDWARE, JACKSONVILLE, FLORIDA

"In *A CEO Only Does Three Things*, Trey Taylor reminds us that nothing in business is more powerful than a focused CEO. This remarkable new book introduces us to Taylor's philosophy of liberation for CEOs around the world shackled to the job of performing tasks that their teams are paid to do. His radical suggestion that a CEO should do the things that only he or she can do and leave the rest to others will strike some as too good to be true. Those of us who have applied his methodology know just how right he is, though. This book should be on every CEO's desktop and nightstand."

—GEORGE ROBBINS, VISTAGE INTERNATIONAL, AND FORMER CEO,
MILLENNIUM SPECIALTY CHEMICALS, JACKSONVILLE, FLORIDA

"*The first book to explain critical concepts of executive leadership in a way that we can learn and remember when our focus wavers. Taylor's A CEO Only Does Three Things provides immediately actionable insights that CEOs can use today! I'd consider it a must-read for leaders in business strategy, corporate development, and corporate alliances.*"

—JIM BLACHEK, CEO, DYNAMIC BENEFIT
SOLUTIONS, WILKES-BARRE, PENNSYLVANIA

"*Trey's ideas in A CEO Only Does Three Things are creative, unique, and transformative. There isn't a platitude in the whole book. It's filled with dynamic business ideas that are simple but profound. I don't know a single executive who wouldn't benefit from being reminded of the core job. This useful book reveals and reminds us of the fundamental laws of management and leadership that lead to success.*"

—TOM PURCELL, CEO, ASHFORD ADVISORS, ATLANTA, GEORGIA

"*By my count, you'd have to read hundreds of books, attend hours of lectures, and engage in limitless conversations to get all the information that my rockstar friend, Trey Taylor, so effortlessly distills into A CEO Only Does Three Things. It's like a lifehack handbook for CEOs to find more time in their day, lead their teams to great results, and make a meaningful impact on the business world.*"

—ERIC SILVERMAN, FOUNDER, VOLUNTARY
DISRUPTION, TOWSON, MARYLAND

A CEO ONLY DOES THREE THINGS

A CEO ONLY

DOES

THREE THINGS

FINDING YOUR FOCUS
IN THE C-SUITE

—

TREY TAYLOR

A BOARD ᴏꜰ ADVISORS BOOK

COPYRIGHT © 2020 TREY TAYLOR

All rights reserved.

A CEO ONLY DOES THREE THINGS

Finding Your Focus in the C-Suite

ISBN   978-1-5445-1725-4 *Hardcover*

       978-1-5445-1727-8 *Paperback*

       978-1-5445-1726-1 *Ebook*

CONTENTS

ACKNOWLEDGMENTS

"The only people with whom you should try to get even are those who have helped you."

—JOHN E. SOUTHARD

This book is a synthesis of a lifetime's worth of ideas encountered while studying the art and science of executive action. I don't pretend that the ideas presented here are original to me; on the whole, they aren't. They've been lifted, tested, and applied in my own career and those of my consulting clients. My peculiar intellectual gift has always been to discover, digest, and synthesize big ideas into usable frameworks. This book is nothing more than that. It would never have seen the light of day without the support and encouragement of many other People, and acknowledging them is the honor of a lifetime.

- To Eddie and Mary Taylor, my parents, for a loving home,

supportive environment, and constant knowledge that you were in my corner through every fight;

- To Roy Taylor, Sr., my grandfather, who first showed me the true value of wealth and hard work, and taught hard lessons with a firm hand;

- To Trent Taylor, my brother and partner for many years, who provided love and support against anyone he didn't think had my best interests at heart;

- To Sheya, Ret, and Emmaline, who share me so selflessly with others, trusting that I have the best interests of the family at heart during all the long nights away working on the book and with clients;

- To Ron Willingham, a mentor of the highest order who put lenses in my intellectual spectacles that allowed me to see People as they really are;

- To my work family, William Hall, Tom Dorywalski, Pete Caucci, Robert Rodriguez, Chris Carpenter, and all of those very special People who come to work each day, executing our mission and allowing me to tinker and experiment;

- To George Robbins's Vistage group, Tom Carroll, Brad Whitchurch, Paul Kassab, Clinton Beeland, Todd Froats, and Jerry Daniels, who stuck with me as I synthesized the ideas into a compact form for others to digest;

- To the graduates of my first CEO Academy, particularly Deb Ault and Jim Blachek, who took the ideas to heart and are building great organizations.

Section I

—

THE ESSENTIALS

FOREWORD

FINDING YOUR FOCUS
IN THE C-SUITE
By Kevin Harrington,
Original *Shark Tank* "Shark"

The path to becoming a CEO is not always a direct one. It's true that for some, it's a natural progression up the corporate ladder, a result of carefully strategized career moves, skillful negotiations, and well-timed successes that lead to the ultimate promotion. Others find themselves in the role as a result of pure serendipity—being in the right place at the right time with the right skillset to serve the needs of the organization as its chief executive. Still others take on the role by virtue of being the only one with the talent to do so, or by founding an enterprise and having a default need for the position to be filled by someone.

In my own life, as a boy growing up in a blue-collar Ohio family, I started selling newspapers on the street at the age of nine and launched my first business at fifteen—sealing driveways in the hot summer sun. It was hard work, but if I complained my dad would say, "Kevin, you'd better make this work. You can't work for anyone else, so you'd better find a way to work for yourself!" I took his advice to heart and graduated to selling baby high chairs door-to-door. I read everything I could to be a better entrepreneur, not understanding that I was really training myself to be a better CEO. I read Napoleon Hill, Zig Ziglar, and anything else successful People told me to read. As I soaked up this wisdom, my personal and business growth began to skyrocket. By my first year in college, I had built my first million-dollar enterprise. I invested in another company, which turned into a $500 million per year business on the New York Stock Exchange and drove the stock price from one dollar to twenty dollars per share. After selling my interest in that company, I formed a joint venture with the Home Shopping Network, called HSN Direct, which grew to hundreds of millions of dollars in sales. Those successes led me to scale the heights of the business world. Some have called me the "father of the infomercial," as I worked to turn television dead air into advertising opportunities and created brands like Ginsu Knives, Tony Little, As Seen on TV, and many others. Along the way, I realized that there was a need in the entrepreneurial community for shared learning, partnership opportunities, and mutual support between business owners. With that in mind, I became a co-founder of EO, The Entrepreneurs' Organization. EO is a global business network of fourteen thousand-plus leading entrepreneurs in 198 chapters and sixty-one countries. Eventually, I was approached to appear on the hit ABC television show *Shark Tank*, as one of the original Sharks.

During my journey I've had highs and I've had lows. I've always been a hustler and always wanted to work hard on the next deal, the next opportunity. The struggle has been worth it, but it has been a *struggle*. When I read *A CEO Only Does Three Things*, I realized that, like many of you, I was spending much of my time as CEO on tasks better left to others, and that was only adding to the struggle.

No matter the path that brings you to the role, each CEO faces the same question once the door to his office closes: what do I do next? As Trey says in this book, the answer is "Focus." It's the most important skill a CEO can have. Where should CEOs focus their attention? On those select areas where our unique skills, experience, reputation, and authority can have the biggest impact on the long-term success or our endeavors. For every company in every industry, three areas are critical: Your People. Your Culture. Your Numbers. Each is connected to the others. Taken together, they act as the foundation upon which your company will build and maintain its success.

The 2017 documentary *Becoming Warren Buffett* recounts the

story of the first time Bill Gates, founder of Microsoft, and Warren Buffett, the CEO of Berkshire Hathaway, met. It was at the home of Gates's parents, who had assembled a group of high achievers, intellectuals, and influencers from all walks of life. Gates's mother, Mary, asked the guests to write down the one thing each of them felt had made them successful. Gates and Buffett had the same answer: "Focus."

Focus is best defined as the ability to select one area of work from among a host of other areas competing for your time and attention. For Trey Taylor, the best CEOs are those with the ability to focus on the three most important areas of their business, while muting all other distractions. It's a question of insight, and in practice, one of prioritization.

The world is swimming in choices today. A recent article announced that Starbucks now offers eighty thousand possible drink options. There are now over 150 flavors of Oreo cookies including such exotic flavors as Green Tea, Red Velvet, Banana Split, and even Swedish Fish! The average American household now receives 189 television channels, as well as access to Hulu, Netflix, Amazon, and YouTube. In any given year, there are roughly four hundred thousand new books published in the English language. During my time on *Shark Tank*, I saw over five hundred pitches for products and businesses, more deals than some see in a lifetime.

CEOs face even more choices. Do I hire this person or that

person? Do I expand into a new product segment, or focus on dominating the categories in which I'm already doing well? Do I grow through acquisition, partnership, or cut-throat sales strategies? And these choices invariably mean making choices for other People too. It's a heavy load.

To capture the challenges that come with so many choices, psychologists have recently coined a new term—"over-choice"—to describe the cognitive problems that come from too many choices prompting too many decisions, most of which have no relative material importance. In studying the effects of overchoice, researchers noted that the presence of prolonged exposure to a high quantity of variables in decision-making seriously affected the quality of those decisions. In other words, the more decisions we have to make over the course of a day, the worse decisions we make at the end of the day. Our ability to make good decisions decreases over time when we are making too many decisions that don't have to be made. To prove the point, think of what you watched on television before bed last night. Did you really want to watch it, or did your decision-fatigue convince you to settle for something barely good enough to keep you from changing the channel?

Across multiple academic studies, one recommendation came through to solve the problem of decision-fatigue: make fewer choices. As you read *A CEO Only Does Three Things*, you'll discover that the great CEOs are those who realize that their capacity for making high-quality decisions that impact the trajectory of their companies is a finite and precious resource. They refuse to waste their brainpower on things that have only temporary or low-level meaning. For this reason, Steve Jobs famously wore the same black turtleneck, blue jeans, and New Balance sneakers every day. It quickly became his trademark look. Mark Zuckerberg, Elizabeth Holmes, and others have adopted this habit as well. But is deciding what to wear every day really that taxing?

Instead of making fewer choices, CEOs have to make the right choices consistently. This means being disciplined about what it is we work on, before allowing our focus to be siphoned away to still-important but less-critical items. That is where this book comes in. Trey Taylor has distilled all of the things that CEOs have to do down into three simple categories: Culture, People, and Numbers. Between the extremes of overchoice and fewer choices, my friend Trey has staked out a middle path that, as CEOs, we can all follow to find success.

As the CEO, you are asked to invest your attention in many things that are important to some People in your organization, but not as important to the organization as a whole. Perhaps your controller has spent months comparing the benefits of switching to a new accounting system for the company and wants your input. Maybe your Human Resources staff wants you to decide between October or

November for your annual benefits enrollment. It could be that Sales has a new compensation plan that needs blessing. Arguably each of these things affects everyone in the company at some tangential level, but does the CEO have some innate knowledge that makes his opinion on the decision better than someone else's?

Being the CEO of an enterprise shouldn't be like being a catcher on a baseball team. Not everything that happens in the company should pass through your inbox. In addition to creating needless delay, this type of decision-making process destroys the quality of the decisions you should be making. To free ourselves from this trap, we need a lens through which to evaluate what decisions belong at the CEO level, and which should be left to others.

The decisions the CEO should make are those that only he has the ability, information, and vision to make. In other words, if a decision can be made by others, it should be. In working with dozens of companies over the years, Trey saw that there are three areas where the CEO has a singular role to play as the head of the company: decisions involving the culture of the company, who works for the company, and what goals the company pursues. All other decisions should be delegated to those People who are closest to the problem being solved. A CEO should invest time in them only when an impasse has arisen.

It sounds simple, but putting it into place is what the rest of this book is about. Whether you are a new CEO trying to figure out how to make sense of chaotic workdays, or a veteran of the C-Suite trying to reignite your passion in the role, this book is for you—but only if you are prepared to make the significant choice it presents. I hope you enjoy reading *A CEO Only Does Three Things* as much as I did. It's the kind of book that I wish had been available when I was a young, up-and-coming CEO, and one whose wisdom I use every day in my business.

INTRODUCTION

MY STORY

In 2005, I had just succeeded in landing my dream job. Five years earlier, internet startup AOL had purchased media giant Time Warner in the biggest merger in history to date with promises of synergies and financial returns that never materialized. A few years into the merger, the combined company had reached a crisis point. In order to survive and deliver on its financial promises, the company would have to shed some of the 250-plus companies it had purchased in its storied past. Assets with powerful brands like *Time* magazine, *Life* magazine, Warner Brothers movies, Netscape, CNN, MapQuest, and MovieFone were all on the chopping block as the gigantic corporation sought to unlock operational capital anywhere it could find it. As the newest member of the Business Affairs team, I was tasked with developing the strategy that would realize $1 billion in cash from selling off assets no longer considered core to the operations of the world's largest media company. I was ready for the challenge.

I had attended Tulane Law School in New Orleans and focused on complex corporate transactions, negotiations, and tax law. I had a special gift for dissecting the inner workings of complex deals, and when others would go glassy-eyed over the minutiae, I would only get more interested. Before joining AOL, I had languished in a poorly run competitor company where the CEO wasn't confident in his abilities, lacked focus, hired consultants to do anything important, and empowered his subordinates to be bullies. I was ready to do meaningful and impactful work in the arena I had staked out for myself.

AOL wanted me to start work immediately, so they bought my house and arranged for a moving truck to head to Atlanta to get my stuff. One morning in January 2005, I got a call from the movers saying, "We're headed your way." Right after I hung up with them I had a call from my mom, "Trey, your dad is in the hospital, it's not looking good, you need to be here now."

My parents had gone to Las Vegas for the New Year to visit family and enjoy the nightlife. Just before they left, my dad had visited the local hospital for chest pains but had erroneously been cleared to go on the trip. The ER doctor stupidly missed the telltale signs of an impending heart attack, and my family paid the price for his negligence when my father passed away a week later. The moving truck never made it to Atlanta. I never took the job with AOL.

Instead, I took over the family business, a financial consulting and insurance firm located in rural Georgia. My only training in running a business was watching others do the job. Now, I had to leave the sidelines, suit up, and get in the game.

Over the next fifteen years, I studied hard, learning everything I could about running a business, leading People, and achieving specific objectives. I joined study groups, masterminds, and advisory boards—a practice I strongly recommend. I actively sought mentors who could teach me what they knew, push me in the right direction, and shape my sense of self—these men and women gave of themselves to better me and my understanding of business in the real world.

As some of those who worked under me will tell you, I messed up a lot. With each failure, I tried to stand up stronger. Always in the back of my mind was the desire to codify all that I learned into a guide I could hand to those who came after me. This book had its genesis in my own need. Brad Montague, the filmmaker behind the Kid President series of YouTube shorts once said, "Be who you needed when you were younger." In that spirit, I wanted to write something that would have helped me find and keep my focus in the most trying of times. My hope is that the ideas, models, and messages presented in this volume do exactly that for someone in need.

TREY TAYLOR

VALDOSTA, GEORGIA

OCTOBER 2020

A CEO ONLY DOES THREE THINGS

"Start by doing what's necessary, then what's possible; and suddenly you are doing the impossible."

—SAINT FRANCIS

Harry Truman famously said, "The buck stops here," and his assertion of accountability has been wildly misinterpreted in American business ever since. What Truman meant by the phrase was that the chief executive of any organization bears the ultimate responsibility for the work done by that organization. What he didn't mean—and this is where so many People get it wrong—is that if no one else is doing the work, it's up to the chief executive to do the work of subordinates. In an entity like the US federal government, this would be akin to asking the President to swab the decks of a battleship because a Seaman is on leave. That idea sounds crazy, but in businesses all over the world, CEOs are constantly doing work to which they bring no value. We are all suffering from a lack of understanding as to the proper role and function of the Chief Executive Officer in American business.

A CEO DOES ONLY THREE THINGS

One of the great venture capitalists of the last thirty years is Fred Wilson. He founded Flatiron Partners, one of the first internet-focused VC firms, as well as Union Square Ventures. Thanks to his genius for spotting concepts that will attract millions of active users, Wilson has led investments in digital enterprises such as Geocities, Twitter, Tumblr, Etsy, Uber, and many others.

Once, before initiating a search for the CEO of a portfolio company that was in trouble after the abrupt departure of its founder, Wilson sought advice from a veteran of the boardroom. "What exactly does a CEO do?" Wilson asked the more experienced man almost rhetorically, looking for something that would help his candidate search.

He wasn't disappointed, as the man answered without hesitation: "A CEO focuses on only three things. He sets the overall vision and strategy of the company and communicates it to all stakeholders. He recruits, hires, and retains the very best talent for the company. He makes sure there is always enough cash in the bank."

In this book, those three focuses are represented by one word each: Culture. People. Numbers. Properly focused, a CEO does these three things and nothing else. Every task of every day should relate directly to improving one of the pillars of this Trinity. Everything that distracts from the Trinity should be delegated to someone else.

When in doubt, let anything that isn't Culture, People, or Numbers slide. These three pillars serve to center your focus on work that must be done. Focusing on them exclusively will clarify and inform your work at a level you've never reached before.

When CEOs of small organizations hear this prescription, they often reject it out-of-hand, scoffing, "That would be great, but right now I'm too busy doing what I have to do to survive." Of course, there is validity to that assertion. After all, startup CEOs who spend all their time navel-gazing about the ideal Culture, or the best possible hire, or what charities they will support once the profits start rolling in, won't be very successful.

But let's state the obvious. Being the CEO is hard; it's three times as hard as the next-hardest job in the organization. A good CEO takes the credit for nothing and the blame for everything. Everyone else in the organization has a right to candor, rapport, and a good night's sleep while the CEO forgoes these for the benefit of the long-term mission. A

CEO is always alone; that's the joy and the hurt of it. As Gordon Gekko proclaims in a memorable scene from the film *Wall Street*, "You win some, you lose some, but you keep on fighting...and if you need a friend, get a dog."

FOCUS AND INTENT

Perhaps things are not quite as dire as the movies depict, but the fact remains that being a CEO means being able to combine two tools that very few People can access: focus and intent. Brad Whitchurch, the CEO of infection control company Seal Shield, defines his role this way: "It's my job to keep the forest in view while tending to the trees." In other words, focus on the tasks at hand but be aware of how those tasks affect the overall health of the business.

If the CEO fails to focus on the three things that matter most—Culture, People, and Numbers—does it mean that the three will go unattended? Unfortunately, no. Aristotle said it best: "Nature abhors a vacuum." Left alone, an asphalt parking lot will break apart, sprout weeds, grow trees, and return to its natural state. The same process is at work in our organizations. If we allow a vacuum to form—a place where executive action does not exist—it will be filled by others, and rarely with the beliefs, actions, and behaviors that lift an organization to new heights.

A CEO's greatest challenge is to tune out the noise by leaving secondary matters to others. Keeping the proper perspective and focusing on the Trinity of Culture, People, and Numbers generates results that can't be achieved otherwise. To accomplish this feat, though, the CEO must form the proper intent.

THE POWER OF INTENT

Every CEO makes decisions. It's central to the job description. What's most important is to make decisions with intent; decisions that matter; decisions whose outcomes have a positive effect on your Culture, People, and Numbers—decisions that propel your business forward.

In her 2007 book *The Intention Experiment*, Lynne McTaggart explored the power of intention. The book closely followed the work of Dr. William Tiller, Professor Emeritus of Materials Science and Engineering at Stanford University. Drawing on the interdisciplinary findings of scientists from around the world, McTaggart concludes that an intent formed in the mind is capable of profoundly affecting the real world. In one experiment, a scientist formed the mental intent to change the pH level of water in a beaker. Over several days of focused thought, he tested the water and found that its reading matched his intended level. In other words, the physical world was affected by the mental world. Tiller says, "For the last 400 years, an unstated assumption of science is that human intention cannot affect what we call physical reality. Our experimental research of the past decade shows that, for today's world and under the right conditions, this assumption is no longer correct."

If Tiller is right and our focused intent can indeed affect our living reality, the implications for CEOs are staggering. Forming and keeping the proper intent with regards to your Culture, People, and Numbers can literally change the world around you. There is an obligation that comes with this knowledge. It isn't enough to just know it; we must put it into practice by incorporating it into our sense of self.

THE PURSUIT OF SELF-KNOWLEDGE

For over three thousand years, Socrates's prescription to "Know thyself" has served as the cornerstone of both Western philosophy and modern psychology. It was inscribed on the entrance to the Temple of Delphi where the Oracle held court and delivered prophecies. For the CEO without recourse to an all-knowing oracle, the concept of self-knowledge takes on special significance. You cannot hope to understand and lead others until you've done the work of understanding yourself.

Without fully understanding what we truly believe—who we are, our fears and aspirations as well as what motivates us—how can we possibly hope to act with intent? If we fail to comprehend our own purpose, how can we hope to comprehend the purpose of our company and our role as CEO? The getting of self-knowledge is a process.

At birth we aren't issued Owner's Manuals with chapters on troubleshooting. Nor can any of today's life coaches or business gurus provide us with instant clarity of our life's purpose and the path to enlightenment. Whatever self-knowledge we want, we will have to get it on our own.

Introspection is one of the most effective ways for the CEO to gain self-awareness. Introspection requires us to examine our thoughts, feelings, and self-image with the goal of identifying what makes us tick. Introspection enables us not only to better understand our motivations but also to determine what is most deserving of our focus.

For leaders, self-awareness is the foundation of self-management and decision-making. The Roman Emperor Marcus Aurelius was perhaps history's most introspective leader. In his classic book *Meditations*, he reminds us that: "These are the characteristics of the rational soul: self-awareness, self-examination, and self-determination."

FOCUS ON THE CAUSES

The life you have today—effortless or challenging, energizing or enervating, profitable or bankrupt—is the outward manifestation of interior causes. These causes are embedded deep within your inner self, and you must discover the beliefs that sustain them. This process takes you deeper into your own psychology than most People ever go, and the results will be profoundly altering. You must tread cautiously here, conscious of the powerful forces at play. Be respectful of them but willing to engage them.

Think on this: through your life experiences—unique to you alone—you have developed deeply rooted, controlling beliefs. With no conscious thought, you make instant, life-shaping decisions about who you are, what capabilities you have, what is possible and not possible for you, and how deserving you are of the success you achieve.

Ron Willingham, the founder and CEO of Integrity Systems, graduated more than 1.5 million People in eighty countries from his personal development courses. A mentor of mine, Willingham recognized that each of us has an internal narrative—he called it our lifescript—and that we live in congruence with that narrative, whether it is accurate or not.

According to Ron, life presents each of us with a series of endless choices. How we make our choices is driven far more by how we see our own story than by any abstract, quantified, or even rational decision-making process. But how many of us ever stop to examine, deconstruct, and rewrite our personal stories? Only by doing so can we ever reach our own authentic selves and be confident in our own choices, choices that are focused on an end goal, directed with proper intent and authentically expressed.

Ron knew that the choices we make form our behaviors, each of which has consequences. Our life then is a summation of the choices we make, the behaviors they engender, and the consequences that result. Knowing this model gives us a tremendous advantage. The model posits a cause-and-effect chain of reactions that determine the quality of life you lead today. Therefore, it makes sense to focus not on the effects but on the causes that produce them.

Doing so, of course, requires a conscious choice to make things better. Making that choice requires an awareness that something isn't right. It may start as a vague feeling that matures into an awareness that things should be better. We can live with that awareness for years before taking action to fix what is wrong. Taking that action means making a choice: do we live with things as they are, or do we commit body, mind, and soul to making them right?

THE PSYCHOLOGY
OF A CEO

"And now here is my secret, a very simple secret: It is only with the heart that one can see rightly; what is essential is invisible to the eye."

—*The Little Prince*, ANTOINE DE SAINT-EXUPÉRY

To lead others, you must understand People—how they tick, how they process information and choose to accomplish certain tasks, what motivates them and why. The greatest executives reach People at their deepest, most fundamental levels. To understand People, we must first understand ourselves and rely on the universal laws of human developmental psychology.

Every person is comprised of three distinct yet interdependent psychological dimensions. Each dimension plays a role in your life, and they work together to bring levels of success consistent with your inner values and self-beliefs. We use the following model to illustrate the point:

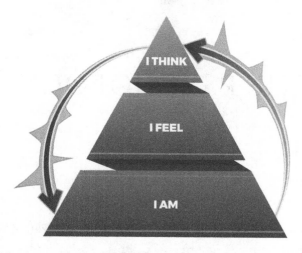

© Lifescript Learning, LLC, 2016

At the top of the pyramid is the "I Think" dimension, the intellectual part of you that learns, makes decisions, and exercises choice. This dimension contains all of the facts and figures you know—what year Columbus sailed to America, your mother's maiden name, how to make toast—and is the repository for most of the formal schooling you receive throughout your life. This dimension operates entirely in the conscious sphere, processing information and giving voice to your inner thoughts. It is largely incapable, however, of propelling you toward action.

In the center of the pyramid is the emotional dimension,

which we label as "I Feel." It is here that your feelings and emotions reside in a semiconscious state. Your entire inventory of possible emotions is stored here, ready to be called upon to initiate you into one of four actions: fight, flight, freeze, or fawn. As a recent Harvard study has confirmed, emotions influence more than 85 percent of your actions and behaviors.[1] In a contest between your "I Think" and "I Feel," your emotions win the day.

The foundation of the pyramid, "I Am," represents the creative dimension that gives rise to your sense of identity. Your values, beliefs, self-image (identity and sense of purpose), and several other powerful psychological mechanisms all reside here in a completely unconscious state. Everything in your life—the quality of your personal relationships, what you allow yourself to achieve, your financial success—finds its genesis in the "I Am" dimension.

This book is designed to build within you the desire and ability to shape your life by focusing on causes, not effects. The Three Dimensions of Human Behavior model is an effective means of doing just that. If you develop an understanding of what you carry inside you and an ability to leverage your positive traits while dispelling your negative ones, how much better will your life be? How much better a CEO will you be?

---

1   Jennifer S. Lerner et al., "Emotion and Decision Making," submitted for publication in the *American Journal of Psychology*, June 16, 2014, https://scholar.harvard.edu/files/jenniferlerner/files/annual_review_manuscript_june_16_final.final_.pdf.

Your "I Think" dimension is in constant interaction with your "I Am" dimension. It scans the world in radar-like fashion, perceiving People, places, and objects, recognizing risks and opportunities, processing any and all stimuli. This dimension is not capable of understanding these stimuli, only collecting them. Because it is in a nonstop conversation with your "I Am" dimension, it constantly asks: "What does this mean? What does this mean? What does this mean?"

Interacting with each other and exchanging information at the speed of light, these two parts of your inner self work to determine the meaning of the world around you and your place therein. When your "I Think" perceives something that your "I Am" contextualizes as positive, then your "I Feel" dimension releases positive emotions to produce the appropriate action. Conversely, negative emotions are released in situations where the "I Am" dimension assigns contextual danger or negativity.

The interactions between the Three Dimensions could make up the curriculum for a master's degree in psychology. We aren't trying to cover that much ground, only to make this important point: whatever you hold in your "I Am" dimension as truth will govern your life. If it governs your life, it will influence your effectiveness as a CEO. If something needs to change, it must first change in your interior self before it can change in the outer world and ultimately transform your business.

THE SECRET TO AUTHENTICITY

We live in an era characterized by the artificial and the insincere. Corporate communications are manufactured by committees of writers, then edited and approved by lawyers. Authenticity is hard to find. From social media posts to company announcements, it becomes harder each day to separate the phony from the real. This is especially true of business leaders who, rather than express their authentic selves, resort to canned statements and shopworn phrases when asked a question that challenges a company policy.

It's not surprising. Much of what has passed for management wisdom teaches that personal belief has nothing to do with the harsh realities of the business world. It says that no matter what the circumstances, managers must be dispassionate, professional, and unemotional. As if any such thing were possible! As if it were desirable!

The world hungers for authenticity. We all want something real in our lives—somewhere safe to place our trust, someone we can believe. Companies will spend millions trying, but you can't buy authenticity. It's an oxymoron!

Authenticity is simple: it is a matter of bringing the Three Dimensions into alignment. In other words, when your beliefs about who you are become mirrored in your thoughts and emotions, you are behaving authentically. Congruence is key; whenever you say, think, feel, or do something that isn't shaped by your beliefs about who you are and what purpose you serve, your authenticity is at risk.

CONNECTING WITH PEOPLE AT THE LEVEL OF BELIEF

Great leaders transcend the intellectual and connect with People at the level of belief (their "I am" dimension). By recognizing and expressing shared values, they show their humanity. They create a common bond to inspire action and contribution. Once so inspired, People can deliver the extraordinary.

All great leaders are driven by a personal vision for their organization. But a personal vision is not enough. Just as artists connect with audiences on a deeper level through paintings, books, or musical compositions, leaders need to tap into the deeper levels of their stakeholders. It's the only way to galvanize them toward a shared goal. To be truly great, a leader must have motivational intelligence.

For CEOs, motivational intelligence can be defined as the ability to understand their own beliefs as well as those of their stakeholders, and to use this understanding to influence stakeholders' thoughts and behaviors.

As previously discussed, gaining self-awareness is the first step. By being self-aware, you are able not only to gauge your emotions but also to leverage your positive traits while overcoming your negative traits. To fully practice this type of intelligence, a CEO must also have the ability to recognize and speak to other People's unconscious motivations. Only by connecting on the deepest level are we able to move People to action.

THE PURSUIT OF SELF-AWARENESS

We all gravitate toward People who are friendly and gregarious—individuals who remember our name and take the time to stop and say hello. When asked to describe such People, we invariably say that they have a great personality. Perhaps, secretly we would like to be like them. In our minds, People with good personalities have an easier time going through life and are almost always successful.

Personality, though, is rarely an indicator of success. A study by the Cornell School of Industrial and Labor Relations found that self-awareness—not personality—is the strongest predictor of a successful career. Being cognizant of your own strengths and weaknesses enables you to work with others who have different skills and experiences. Self-awareness also allows us to more readily accept ideas and perspectives that differ from what we know or think can have value. Conversely, a lack of self-awareness comes off as rigidity, stubbornness, or an intractability that alienates others.

It would be easy to assume that all successful leaders, whether in business or politics, are born with self-awareness, that it is an innate characteristic, something hard-coded into their DNA. But we know that isn't the case.

Organizational psychologist Tasha Eurich finds that, "Ninety-five percent of People believe that they're self-aware, but only about ten to fifteen percent really are."[2] This self-awareness gap is even wider as we climb the ladder of success. Eurich reports that, "The more power a leader holds, the more likely they are to overestimate their skills and abilities. One study of more than 3,600 leaders across a variety of roles and industries found that, relative to lower-level leaders, higher-level leaders more significantly overvalued their skills (compared with others' perceptions). In fact, this pattern existed for nineteen out of the twenty competencies the researchers measured, including emotional self-awareness, accurate self-assessment, empathy, trustworthiness, and leadership performance."

One possible reason for this deficit has to do with status. Like star athletes who hear nothing but praise from fans who want to travel in their orbit, leaders rarely get candid feedback from those around them. No one wants to tell the Emperor he has no clothes. Companies value People

---

2   Tasha Eurich, "What Self-Awareness Really Is (and How to Cultivate It)," *Harvard Business Review*, January 4, 2018, https://hbr.org/2018/01/what-self-awareness-really-is-and-how-to-cultivate-it.

who are positive and "team players." Better to nod and agree than to challenge the accepted wisdom and place your job in jeopardy.

If this is true—and from my experience, it most decidedly is—then the only way the CEO can attain true self-awareness is by analyzing his owns actions with a critical eye. As a CEO, you must do the work that others aren't willing or able to do—critically examining your beliefs and behaviors, and working to optimize them.

Management guru Peter Drucker advises that, "Whenever you make a decision, write down what you expect will happen. Nine or twelve months later, compare the results with what you expected…it's the only way to discover your strengths." Drucker calls this process "feedback analysis." Warren Buffett may be the most famous practitioner of this method. For years, he has written down his reasons for every investment he makes. Later, he compares his decision with the final outcome, noting what worked and what didn't, as well as the validity of his reasoning and the motivations behind it.

The more a CEO works on himself—understanding the internal landscape of his own psychology—the better a leader he can be. It takes a lifetime's worth of work. There are no easy answers, but there are quick wins for those with the foresight and insight to do the hard work of self-assessment and growth.

A TIME FOR
CHOOSING

"Destiny is not a matter of chance; it is a matter of choice. It is not a thing to be waited for, it is a thing to be achieved."

—WILLIAM JENNINGS BRYAN

By and large, CEOs are readers. It's probably why you are holding this book instead of watching a YouTube video on how to be a better a CEO. Statistics show that the typical American reads three books a year, but the average CEO reads twelve. CEOs digest and implement the ideas they find in books. They read more than other People because they want to be better, to do better, to make better decisions.

Decisions are never easy. Rarely is a leader presented with a binary decision: "Should we do this or that?" Rather, every decision involves several options, each of which can appear to be the right choice given the circumstances. Often, the CEO will call upon expert advice, solicit the feedback of the senior management team, or seek the perspective of trusted advisors before making a decision. But ultimately, deciding is what CEOs are paid to do. When it comes to decisions regarding the Trinity of Culture, People, and Numbers, the CEO is the sole and final arbiter. These decisions cannot be delegated. The chief executive must own the consequences of these decisions, whether they are good or bad.

An ocean of ink has been spilled discussing what separates a good decision from a poor one. While we won't review all of that information, there are two universal factors that define poor decisions. First, when we make decisions without reference to our core beliefs of right and wrong—our values—the decision will be a poor one, regardless of whether it's technically correct or not. For example, maybe I'm facing tremendous pressure from a competitor. I've done everything I can to best him in the marketplace, and I feel that spreading lies and slander is now my only option, despite my core belief in truth as a defining value of my life. As soon as I tell the first lie, I've acted against my core values and made a poor decision, and its weight will be with me until I acknowledge and make amends for it.

Second, and far more prevalent, when we make a decision without the commitment to carry it through to success, we've made a poor decision. The Stoic philosopher Epictetus encapsulates this truth in his *Enchiridion*, teaching that:

Tentative efforts lead to tentative outcomes. Therefore, give yourself fully to your endeavors. Decide to construct your character through excellent actions and determine to pay the price of a worthy goal. The trials you encounter will introduce you to your strengths. Remain steadfast...and one day you will build something that endures: something worthy of your potential.

CROSSING THE RUBICON

In 49 BC, Julius Caesar marched his army to the banks of the Rubicon, a small Italian river that marked the northern border of the Roman Republic. Caesar had spent nearly a decade away from his privileged place in the Eternal City conquering Gaul (modern-day France) while extending Roman hegemony from Germany and the isle of Britain. By virtue of his success as a general, Caesar awaited the Senate's award of a Triumph, the highest honor accorded to Roman citizens.

A Triumph provided a victorious general an unmatched forum for self-promotion as well as an opportunity to gain popularity with the Roman mob. At the end of a week-long celebration in which the spoils of war were displayed and divided among the People, the general mounted a gilded chariot, his face painted red with vermilion in imitation of Mars, the god of war, a crown of oak leaves on his head. As he rode down the Via Sacra—the city's central avenue— thronged with citizens shouting his praise, a lone slave stood behind him in the chariot repeating, "You are a man. You are no god. You serve Rome."

A Triumph was the pinnacle of life for a Roman, and Caesar and his troops had earned it. But it was not to be. A herald from the Senate was sent to Caesar on the banks of the Rubicon, bearing instructions from the Roman Senate: "Disband your army and proceed to Rome to answer charges against you in the Senate. Do not cross the River with your men under arms. There will be no Triumph for you or your army. You will not be allowed to stand for Consul." The Senate ended the message with the incendiary phrase: "Fear this and tremblingly obey."

Caesar dismissed the messenger with dignity and respect and promised an answer the following day at sunrise. The rest of the evening, he walked the banks of the Rubicon alone with his thoughts. When dawn broke, the messenger sought Caesar in his General's tent only to discover that Caesar was supervising the army's crossing of the river into Italy. Giving his answer to the messenger, Caesar called out "Alea jacta est!" or "The die is cast!" a phrase used by Roman soldiers to signal the beginning of a game. He then put spurs to his horse and crossed the river.

Caesar's decision to cross the Rubicon appears logical. He was a victorious general returning home to claim the rewards that were now denied him. Who would stand against him? Who indeed!

On the other side of the river stood the full might of Rome, the most powerful state in the world. The Senate—the oldest, richest, and most powerful men of the Republic—united against Caesar. Rome's most famous general, Pompeius Magnus (Pompey the Great), once Caesar's son-in-law and political partner, and arguably his superior in both influence and military accomplishment, led the opposition.

To crush Caesar, the Senate directed Pompey to raise an army of 130,000 soldiers by recruiting as many men as possible from the provinces. Whatever money was needed to put men under arms would come from the public treasury and from the private wealth of the senators. Contributions were also to be levied from the allied and subjugated cities of the Republic.

In contrast, Caesar had brought with him just one legion consisting of five thousand men. But despite his enemies' overwhelming advantage in both wealth and men, Caesar was able to draw upon an inner trait that neither Pompey nor the Senate possessed: decisiveness.

The Senate expected Caesar to send for reinforcements from Gaul before advancing against the City. Rather than allowing his enemies to gain a numerical advantage that he had no chance of overcoming, Caesar entered Italy while the Senate was still debating its options and Pompey was recruiting troops. Caesar's speed and boldness shocked the Senate, and when his legion sounded the ram's horn to announce its arrival in Rome, the Senate and Pompey fled to the countryside, eventually taking refuge in Egypt 1,500 miles away, leaving Caesar the undisputed master of Rome.

Was Caesar's decision to cross the Rubicon an impulsive move that worked out thanks to a stroke of luck? Or was his audacity born of something deeper?

Caesar believed himself to be a man of fate. To be accorded a Triumph was his right not only as a victorious general but as a distinguished member of the Julian clan, descended from gods and kings. To deny him this right was not only an affront to his military accomplishments but to his very identity. Looking deep within, Caesar saw himself as one destined for greatness. Throughout his life, every action he took was a step toward achieving this goal. For Caesar, crossing the Rubicon and engaging those who would deny him his birthright was not only logical but preordained and inevitable.

Just like Caesar, we all have difficult decisions to make. Will the decisions you make reflect your personal beliefs and values? Will you become the CEO your company deserves? The choice is yours. Choose wisely.

Section II

—

CULTURE

CULTURE TRUMPS
EVERYTHING

"Culture eats strategy for breakfast."

—PETER DRUCKER

As we've learned, each person working for a company has an individual view of themselves and how they fit into the world at large. Our self-images, or identities, form the basis for our judgments, behaviors, and responses to challenges and opportunities. Just as this is true for People, it's also true for companies which are, at the most basic level, collections of People. Corporate identity is best expressed by its Culture.

A CEO only does three things, and Culture is one of them. A primary role of the CEO is to align corporate Culture with the underlying shared values of its People. While sometimes daunting, this goal is far from unprecedented. Throughout history, leaders of every stripe and caliber have been challenged to understand themselves and the societies in which they lived. Only by bringing the two into accord were they able to build something lasting and unique.

YOUR MOST IMPORTANT COMPETITIVE ADVANTAGE

When you take inventory of what makes your business successful, you might look first to the quality of your products, then to the sophistication of your internal processes, and maybe even to your intellectual property portfolio of patents and trademarks. Some CEOs identify the team of People supporting the company's mission as a prime contributor to success. Increasingly, though, CEOs around the world have come to understand that a company's Culture is its most important competitive advantage.

An overwhelming 82 percent of the respondents to Deloitte's "Global Human Capital Trends" survey said they believe that Culture is a potential competitive advantage. And yet, most employers struggle to build a vibrant company Culture. The same survey found that only 12 percent of executives believe their companies are building the "right culture," and just 19 percent believe that their company currently has the "right culture."[3]

---

3   "Global Human Capital Trends 2016," Deloitte University Press, accessed September 10, 2020, https://www2.deloitte.com/content/dam/Deloitte/global/Documents/HumanCapital/gx-dup-global-human-capital-trends-2016.pdf.

This realization—that Culture plays a paramount role in a company's lifecycle—has been a long time coming. There are many CEOs today who still overlook or underestimate the value of Culture. Establishing, shaping, and nurturing a Culture is profound and impactful work of the highest order, and only the CEO can oversee it. Those who mire themselves in the day-to-day minutiae of the business never get to experience the state of flow that comes from a high-functioning Culture.

The roots of Culture touch every corner of your business. When Culture thrives, you attract talented People who perform exceptionally on behalf of the business, which in turn drives positive growth in your Numbers. When a company's Culture is broken, your best People move on to other opportunities, and the People who stay are unlikely to act in the business's best interests; execution and even profits will eventually falter.

Intuitively, we know that Culture is important. Yet, because cultural problems never present themselves directly—only through the behaviors of your People and the results of behaviors—they are often harder to nail down and address than other business challenges. For this reason, you must train yourself to think of Culture as a contributing factor to every challenge and every success you face in business. Each day you must seek to understand the cultural antecedents of the tasks that fill your inbox, because they are there, and often go unaddressed.

WHAT IS COMPANY CULTURE?

The most important words in any language—like "Culture"—are those that are so basic that defining them is a challenge. Imagine explaining the concept of romantic love to someone whose native language has no direct cognate for the term. How would you begin to define something so basic and fundamental to the way you experience the world?

In defining your company's Culture, you face a similar task. In literal terms, Culture has three divergent meanings:

- There is Culture as a process of individual enrichment; we say that certain People are "Cultured" because they have invested time in adopting refined manners and interesting habits;
- There is Culture as a group's particular way of life, such as when we talk about French Culture or Native American Culture;
- Finally, there is Culture as a set of activities: visiting museums, going to concerts, reading books, watching movies, etc.

These three definitions of Culture are quite different, and they can compete with one another. Every time we use the word Culture, we subtly incline toward one of its aspects: toward the Culture that's passively obtained through osmosis or the Culture that's learned actively and with much effort; toward the Culture that makes you a better a person, or the

Culture that indicates your identity as a member of a group. Recognizing the difference between the three meanings enables you to use them all. Looking deeper, we can use the etymology of the word to shed some light on its meaning.

The original use of the word Culture comes to us from Latin, where the verb "colere" means "to tend and care for, to cultivate, to encourage by preparation of outside conditions." So, in its original form, Culture was the result of what you cared about.

Today, the concept of Culture goes far beyond its definitions, and its relevance to your business should be immediately clear. Culture is the ethical environment in which we live and work, including the beliefs, behavioral rules, traditions, and rituals that bind us together. Every group of People forms a Culture—a summary of what we agree is the right way to act toward one another based on our shared beliefs. If you can get a grasp on a group's Culture, you will soon find that it's a better predictor of future behavior than biology or personality.

Think about it this way: We all have that one friend—loud, boisterous, big personality—who fills the whole room with his presence. We love him for who he is. When you take him to a party, he knows everyone's name within ten minutes. What happens, though, when you take him to the symphony? Does the strings section know him by name? Does he give the French horn player a fist bump? Or does he change his actions to match those of everyone else in the audience?

Culture trumps everything. It trumps personality; it trumps biology; it trumps our previous education and training. Culture trumps everything because Culture drives behavior. It is unspoken, automatic, and almost invisible. Culture helps us determine what we should or should not do in a given situation. This is what makes Culture crucial to business: the CEO cannot be physically available to influence every choice that every employee has to make each day. But Culture can.

Culture is the water in which we swim, and just like fish, we usually don't know that it is there. The CEO's role is to care for the Culture. To nurture it so that it is fresh and healthy. Otherwise, dangerous parasites will invade the pond.

A TALE OF TWO CULTURES

A Culture exists in your company, and it does not matter if you designed it or if it came from a three-day retreat entitled "The Way We Work." It doesn't matter if you talk about it. It doesn't matter if you are conscious of it, because others are. It's there.

Your company's Culture can either be the result of deliberate choice, driven by your decisions as the CEO and championed by your People, or it can be the collective result of the unguided, unmonitored choices of your People. Culture is like a plot of land. If you plant and water crops, you can grow a lush garden. If you leave the plot unattended, weeds will overrun the property. No matter what, something will grow. That's how Culture works.

Cultures fall into two categories:

- Least Common Denominator—These Cultures are accidental at best, determined by what members do and how leadership reacts, making them fragile and fluid. They break easily and always take the form of whatever certain employees feel is best for them. Clients take a backseat in these Cultures, and so do the best interests of the business. No mountains are climbed, and no records are broken.
- Intentional—CEOs who take the time to be intentional about their company's core ideology are the unsung heroes of the American business landscape. They commit themselves to working every day to ensure that positive cultural values are personified in every employee. Their work is not produced; it is breathed into life. In an intentional Culture, employees make choices aligned with business and client interests.

Culture exists whether you want it to or not. If you are intentional about fostering and nurturing your Culture, you can use it as an accelerant for growth, pushing your company to greater heights. If you are unintentional about your Culture, a least-common-denominator Culture will fill the void.

Your choice as a CEO is to either ignore your Culture, which allows weeds to choke your crops, or to invest in the intentional practice of tending and caring for the farm, giving your plants the nutrients and support they need to flourish. This is your garden. What will you plant?

THE ETHICAL ENVIRONMENT IN WHICH YOU LIVE

Your Culture—the ethical environment in which you live— may be automatic in its formation. No one gets up in the morning and says, "Today I will find three like-minded individuals who believe the same sacred and fundamental truths about ethics and fairness as I do. I will build a substantial part of my life around them, and they will do the same around me. We will achieve great things because of this symbiotic relationship."

And yet we do this unconsciously by filtering People in and out of our lives based on the nano-signaling that happens at the neuronic level in our brains. We are hardwired to seek out those who are similar to us and to attract them to us in the same way. It seems accidental, and when it works out, it's called serendipity.

In contrast, when a Culture becomes polluted and toxic, formed for the wrong motivations, or allowed to be corrupted by new members who hold different viewpoints, it can be a scarring psychological experience for those involved. Polluted water affects every fish in the tank.

The same is true for us. If our Cultures become toxic, the poison will affect each of our People. Left unchecked, past the point of a cure, each relationship in the group can die and the Culture will cease to be recognizable. Our task then is to be proactive enough to ensure a clean tank at all times, and reactive enough to remove the toxins when we find them.

We know that there are three dimensions of human behavior and they exist beyond the individual sphere. Businesses have these same three dimensions, and an effective Culture aligns each of them into a coherent and congruent framework in which everyone participates. This alignment comes in part from how you personally model correct and desirable behaviors, and in part from those you recruit to join you on the journey.

CEOs cannot institute a Culture through decree, but they do have the ability to affect and shape one over time. Intentionally building a Culture that brings to life the most closely held values of its adherents is an exciting opportunity.

YOUR VALUES
PROPOSITION

"Your beliefs become your thoughts,
Your thoughts become your words,
Your words become your actions,
Your actions become your habits,
Your habits become your values,
Your values become your destiny."

—GANDHI

Henry Ford believed in the power of money and the power of People. But for a belief to be more than words, he also knew it had to be put into action. That's what he did when he was confronted with employee turnover.

A little background: In 1913, Henry Ford introduced the moving assembly line at his plant in Highland Park, Michigan. The innovation worked better than expected, with production of the company's Model T motorcar nearly doubling. The trouble was that the assembly line's monotonous, repetitive work was causing workers to quit in droves.

Ford decided to take radical action. As a first step, the Ford Motor Company would reduce the workday from nine hours to eight. It would also expand to three shifts a day instead of two, thereby creating jobs. But the biggest shock came when Ford announced that he would more than double the basic rate of pay to five dollars a day. This translated to an additional annual investment of $10 million to improve the lives of his workers.

It was the best investment Ford ever made. Within a year, turnover fell from 370 percent to 16 percent. Over the same period, productivity rose to 70 percent, which enabled the company to reduce the Model T's price from around $800 to $350. Commenting on the pay raise and its subsequent benefits, Henry Ford told reporters: "We believe in making twenty thousand men prosperous and contented rather than follow the plan of making a few slave drivers in our establishment millionaires."

FROM INTENT TO CULTURE

As we have learned, our intent has the power to affect even the physical world. Forming a Culture may happen by chance, but only by continually curating, cultivating, and grooming it will we get the results we want. This is what makes our Culture show up in the daily behaviors of our People.

Henry Ford could have done nothing when his assembly line made work at his company monotonous and boring. But if he hadn't done something, someone else would have. Most likely, disgruntled employees would have further spread the seeds of discontent. Instead, Ford put his beliefs into action, demonstrating to his workers that he understood and shared their concerns about the physical work environment he had created.

If you don't curate your Culture, someone else will, and the results will be the very thing you do not want—a least-common-denominator Culture. An abundance of research underscores what happens when this type of Culture develops. Gallup's 142-country report on the "State of the Global Workplace" reveals that almost two-thirds of employees are not engaged at work, while 25 percent are actively disengaged and focused on other tasks, leaving only one in seven positively engaged in their work.

It doesn't have to be that way. Statistics from New Century Financial Corporation indicate that employees who are actively engaged in their jobs are more productive. While this may come as no surprise, the impact of employee engagement might shock you. Companies with engaged employees outperform the competition by 20 percent, earn more than their competitors, and rank above industry benchmarks in almost all categories.

According to a 2019 report from PricewaterhouseCoopers, two factors contribute to the problem, and one thing combats it. When managers and executives fail to adequately communicate expectations that are grounded in principle, employees mentally unplug until they more clearly understand objectives. And when a company's pace and cadence is oriented toward only short-term goals, employees never feel a sense of accomplishment.[4] The antidote to lack of engagement is a focus on Culture.

Many executives polled in these studies admitted that while they knew Culture was important, they didn't know how to build one. It can be a daunting task, but conceiving of your Culture as the operation system on which your business runs is a helpful concept.

A Cultural operating system consists of basic rules, norms, and procedures that support your vision for the right kind of Culture to fit your organization. As in any computer system, you must start by defining what is true. All computer languages have their roots in the binary system of 0's and 1's, 0 always equals 0 and 1 always equals 1. These are universal

---

4   "The 2019 Transparency Report," PwC, accessed September 10, 2020, https://www.pwc.com/us/en/about-us/pwc-llp-transparency-report.html.

throughout the system and constant in their operations. So too must we have universals and constants in our cultural operating system.

The Ritz-Carlton organization—synonymous with high-class, high-touch service—calls its cultural operating system the "Gold Standards." Every Ritz employee carries a card that contains its motto: "We are ladies and gentlemen serving ladies and gentlemen." This motto is supported by the organization's Three Steps of Service Philosophy, Twelve Service Values, and Employee Promise. Every day, Ritz-Carlton employees around the globe—thousands of People in more than ninety hotels in twenty-seven countries—gather for five-minute meetings in small groups called Daily Line-Ups. In these huddle-style meetings, they review one of the Twelve Service Values. That's a cultural operating system in action!

In my own company, we have thirteen "Be Attitudes" that express what we believe and how we want to be measured when putting our beliefs into actions. They serve as guideposts when we don't know the way, and as yardsticks when we evaluate our actions. Every meeting starts with a discussion of that week's Be Attitude, and every project must be connected to at least three of our core values before we consider it a corporate priority. In this way we keep our daily work rooted in our values.

Intentional acts have more thrust behind them because they

are fueled by the power of belief. Belief stems from the values we hold dear, the emotional fuel they bring to our everyday activities, and our desire to live in congruence with those things we think are right. When we employ our intention to cultivate our Cultures, important things happen. The sum total of these intentional actions serves to establish our cultural operating systems.

To design the Culture that you want for your company, you must take inventory of the shared values of the group. What are those things that you and your team believe to be universally true? Those are the things that you care about most, the things that you seek in your lives. They are your values.

Values are personally rooted in each person's "I Am" dimension. Collectively, they permeate your entire organization. Just as values are the foundation of our individual belief systems, so too do they form the foundation of our Culture. Tapping into the shared values identity of a group of People gives you tremendous power to influence the group's behaviors.

Your values may be entirely conscious, entirely unconscious, or somewhere on the spectrum between those two poles. The first step to building a world-class Culture is to make your values conscious by articulating them intentionally. The mental work necessary to carefully reflect on your most closely held beliefs will pay dividends as the clarity of your statements releases excitement and energy into your organization.

STEP #1: CONDUCTING A VALUES ASSESSMENT

The first step in articulating your Culture is to take inventory of the Culture's primary values. Your task is to think about the behaviors members of your team exhibit. Behaviors are the physical evidence of personal or group values, upon which individually model their actions. Behaviors point the way to the closely held values of a Culture.

You'll want to play the part of the detective, observing from a distance, maintaining your objectivity and watching to see what behaviors show up. Use all your faculties to gain the broadest possible understanding of your Culture. You won't have to eavesdrop or spy on your People to observe their behaviors, but you may need to adjust your mindset to take it all in. This is not a time for judgment, only an opportunity to observe.

- Watch how People handle personal transitions in your group. Are birthdays, work anniversaries, promotions, and milestones marked and celebrated with enthusiasm?
- Do your People show up to work on time and primed for productivity? Are deadlines met?
- Do your People socialize outside of work?
- Listen to the voice of your company. What phrases pop

up most often in conversations about work? How do your People describe the company and their roles in it? How do they perceive customers? What do these verbal behaviors say about your Culture?

- Look closely at how People decorate their workspaces. Do you see motivational posters, pictures of family and pets, favorite quotes? Are there rules posted everywhere: how to brew coffee, when to throw out food in the break room refrigerator, how cool the air conditioning can be? What do these visual behaviors say about your Culture?

Next, involve your team. Facilitate a high-level discussion in which each person is encouraged to give voice to the most important behaviors they see at your company. Do not share your list but instead lead the team in brainstorming theirs. Give them some prompts, like: "I like that we _____," and "We always _____," or "We are known for _____." As each person shares, thank them for the idea and resist the urge to consolidate or combine ideas; let each submission live on its own for now. As with all brainstorming sessions, having a fixed time limit will yield better results. Set a timer and keep the feedback quick and the discussion minimal.

Be wary if the discussion takes a negative turn. People sometimes use this exercise as an opportunity to vent dissatisfaction, and that isn't its purpose. At this stage, you only want to capture those values that are true and desirable in your company.

Ultimately, you will have two lists: the one you made and the one your team compiled. Examine them side by side. Do you and your People see your Culture through the same lens? What insights present themselves in the contrast between the two lists? Are there areas of overlap?

Typically, this exercise will yield between ten and thirty behaviors. Examine each behavior and determine what underlying belief gives rise to it. Beliefs that drive behaviors, we call values. List your values, consolidating where you see overlap.

In compiling your list, recognize that your values are not those things that you perform with perfection 100 percent of the time. They can be aspirational and include things that you reach for and sometimes fall short of. That said, the list shouldn't be a wish list on which you note what you want to be true but isn't. With practice, you can develop a dynamic tension between what is true, and what is becoming true.

This is where most value systems start to fail. Corporate values and mission statements can easily become ironic commentaries on what a company actually stands for. Let's remember that even Enron—a company now synonymous with fraud and double-dealing—had their core values of Integrity, Communication, Respect, and Excellence chiseled in marble in the corporate lobby. Obviously, the simple act of writing down that your company values integrity does not mean that your employees display it. Rather, your business has to be organized around your values, and you as the CEO have to lead by making choices based on those values.

Taking all of this into account, ask yourself how well your organization manifests your values to the world each day. For each value, ask: "How confident am I that the whole team lives this value every day?" Assign a score between 0 percent and 100 percent.

Now look at the list again. Those values that you grade above 85 percent are the true values of your Culture. Those scoring 75 percent or higher are aspirational—values that only some People follow. They do not currently define your Culture. Any scores below 75 percent are not contributing values to your Culture, but normalized behaviors of a handful of People.

The number of core values you settle on does not matter— some businesses have as few as three, others more than twenty. Focus on cataloging those values that produce the behaviors most necessary for your business's success. In formulating your values, less can be more. Choose the values with the highest scores, those you are certain your company practices, even if that means selecting a lower number of values.

STEP #2: CRAFTING VALUE STATEMENTS

Webster's defines *context* as "the circumstances that form the setting for an event, statement, or idea in terms of which it can be fully understood and assessed." Recently, my firm facilitated a strategic planning workshop for a client. One of the attendees, a young woman new to the client, eagerly participated in the exercise. As the group discussed its closely held values, she suddenly exclaimed in frustration, "That's fine, but what does it mean for me!?" Her outburst was born out of the need for context.

For employees to fully adopt those values that we have identified as governing our Culture, we need to provide enough context so that for each value People understand why and how it is practiced, and the end result it should produce.

It falls to the CEO to complete the values inventory and to give those values refinement, context, and expression. It's not enough to say, "We value truth." Rather, you must craft a statement that illustrates the context surrounding the value. This statement should capture why you have this value as seminal in your Culture. It should illustrate how this value is expressed in the behavior of your People. It should take the form of a mini-mantra that People participating in your Culture can use when issues present themselves and you aren't around to provide guidance. For example, my firm values honesty as a core value and our articulated Be Attitude #7 is:

BE TRUTHFUL

We practice Truth for its own sake. It may be called by many names, but great People recognize that Truth is universal and unchangeable. Honesty, integrity, authenticity, and doing the right thing all carry strong auras of positive influence. Truth defines our firm.

No matter the consequences, we tell the Truth. We do so fiercely when appropriate, gently when called for, but authentically at all times.

We do the right thing, as well as say the right thing.

We know that truth brings courage and confidence.

By articulating the value "Be Truthful" in this way, we clearly communicate what it means to us and how it should influence our work and choices. We designed the value around our business and our People. Your values may be quite different, but the framework should be the same: articulate the value; provide the necessary context; express the behaviors that are associated with that value.

For both you and your company, these values should trigger an emotional response. When I assess values in a workshop format or one-on-one with clients, I often see sincere tears. Values should affect you and your People at a deep level. If they do not, you may have the wrong values or the wrong People. Either way, you have something to fix.

To a large extent, this is a heuristic process of working backward from a desired result to discover its causes. You start with a positive behavior in your workplace Culture, one that you want to be the default action on display at all times. Then you examine that behavior to determine what value or belief lies at its core. Identifying that value gives you the clarity to flesh it out, expand upon it, work the words until it becomes teachable, transferable, and comprehensible to those around you.

I realize that this can be challenging. Do not let it frustrate you. Do not be afraid to go back and revise your value statements to craft the best versions possible. In fact, you should do so. The more work you put into getting the formulation perfect upfront, the more widely accepted and the better activated a given value will be over the long term. The drafting process is complete when the final version provides enough context that someone encountering the value for the first time can understand what behavior your Culture requires.

STEP #3: CHOOSE A THEME

In music theory, a theme is a melodic figure or phrase that forms the basis of a composition. Musical themes are repeated many times in many different formats and by many different voices or instruments, thereby connecting the different parts of the composition into a unified whole. Similarly, your goal as CEO is to create cultural themes that connect the different values you discover into an integrated system of belief and behavior—your cultural operating system.

I work with clients across multiple industries, and the themes of their cultural operating systems are as unique as the Cultures they describe. For example, one of our clients in the entertainment industry describes their values as the "FUNdamentals," with an emphasis on delighting clients and delivering memorable experiences. Another client in the engineering space describes their beliefs as the "Specs" and have written them to read like an engineering specifications document. Still another client in the software industry touts "Source Code" as the theme for its cultural operating system. Another client in the restaurant franchising business shares its "Secret Sauce" with each employee. In each case, the CEO has chosen a relevant theme that speaks to the team and serves to tie the values into a single package.

In completing this step, you must think deeply and originally about your organization. What theme will speak to the team? What will pull them in and keep them engaged? Exercise your creativity and choose a compelling theme that communicates and engages. Develop it from within and frame it in a way that makes sense to you. There are many worthwhile examples to follow, but if you simply duplicate another business's value system, it will not stick. The DNA of the transplant won't match that of the host, and as with a failed organ transplant, your People will reject it. You can learn from others, but your value system has to be developed organically. It must be yours.

What theme best speaks to your concept of your organization's Culture? What related concepts or images suggest themselves when you think about this theme? How might they be deployed to make the theme more attractive to your organization?

Of course, you can design the most compelling theoretical cultural operating system in the world, but if the values enshrined in the Culture aren't yours to live, it will do more harm than good. Make sure that you can endorse every idea in your Culture through your actions and with passionate conviction. Your success as a CEO depends on it.

YOUR COMMITMENT
TO VALUES

"Culture is to recruiting as product is to marketing."

—HUBSPOT'S CULTURE CODE

A CEO must do certain things intentionally for the benefit of everyone in the company, from the receptionist to the CFO. If you do not personally own the responsibility of curating your Culture, someone else will. In this vacuum, the business drifts toward a least-common-denominator Culture where the People making choices about what the company truly values do not have the big-picture vantage point of the CEO. They don't have the impact on People that a CEO does, and they certainly do not see the Numbers the way a CEO does. So, it is impossible for anyone but you to champion and lead Culture.

This means that you must personally act according to your stated values and be accountable to them. When I say this during a speech, the typical reaction is a head nod from the audience. "Of course we are accountable to our own values," they think. In practice, though, we can be just as blind to our unconscious behaviors as anyone in our organization. This can lead to eye-opening and sometimes difficult conversations that challenge your commitment to your values.

We once hired a young intern who later transitioned into an entry-level position. She was intelligent, motivated, and our team agreed that her contributions to projects were positive and worthwhile. You have likely met young People like this in your own organization—eager and capable but in need of some direction. You see their potential, and you appreciate that helping them grow will lead to continued rewards for your business. She might not be leading a board meeting, but a good hire is a good hire at any level.

One day, she knocked on my office door and asked if I had a minute to speak with her. I invited her in, and she launched into a respectful explanation of why we should reverse course on a recent decision I'd made for the company. The implementation work had just begun, and she strongly believed that the direction did not align with our values. She walked through our values, making her case for why each individual value was not well-represented by the new effort.

I sat across from an entry-level employee, listening. I had decades more business experience. I had run the Numbers. I had done the research. I had squared the new plan with our values in my own mind. My team had agreed that the plan was a step forward for the company. By all accounts, there was no reason I should let her tell me how to run my business—she was barely an adult, just out of school. No reason, except for the fact that she was right. In making the change, we had not conducted a basic impact analysis and she caught us red-handed making a choice that would inconvenience our clients.

Our Culture taught her to champion our values—to stand up for them when she felt they were not being respected. It taught her to ground her choices in our values and to have the courage to fight for the right expression of them in our behaviors. Because I had intentionally built a Culture that empowered her, she was able to stand in front of me—nervous but full of passion—and tell me that I was wrong. The Culture we had created overrode all other traditional systems of power and authority.

At that moment, in the face of proof that we were making a mistake, I could have easily let my ego rule the day and ignored the company values. If I had kicked her out of my office for challenging my authority, the message would have been clear to all: we talk about our values, but we don't live them.

Instead, I wanted the message to be that our values—not our egos—determine our behaviors. I thanked her for her courage and for her work. I convened the team and had her make the same presentation to them. Her arguments carried the day. We reversed the pending decision and implemented a superior strategy that otherwise would never have come to light. Culture trumps everything.

In your leadership role, you will face dozens of scenarios like this one. Running a business is a complex task with countless obstacles and pitfalls. You will, at some point, be held accountable to the values by which you ask your own People to live. This is why it is imperative that you get it right from the beginning. Being held accountable to values that you only half-heartedly believe will gut your efforts at a critical time in your business.

BUILDING A CULTURE WITH VALUES

When I was seven years old, I was spending the day with my grandfather, a prominent businessman in our small town. We visited his office, made a deposit at the bank, and stopped in for coffee at the Chamber of Commerce. Around lunchtime, I was hungry and asked for Kentucky Fried Chicken, my favorite. He obliged me and drove to the local KFC, where we met Mr. Owen Harris, the franchisee. He was walking around the parking lot, picking up trash.

My grandfather and Mr. Harris were friends. They did charitable and political work together, so I knew I was in for a long wait as they caught up on the latest news. Halfway through their discussion, Mr. Harris stiffened and ran out into the road in front of his store, scooped up a paper cup with Colonel Sanders on the side of it and ran back, all the time dodging cars. My grandfather and I were astonished. "Owen," my grandfather exclaimed, "You could've been killed just now!" Laughing, Mr. Harris said, "I know it, but I couldn't stand for anyone to think we had thrown that cup in the road."

Thirty-five years later, I recounted that story at Mr. Harris's funeral as our community gathered to celebrate a life dedicated to the pursuit of excellence and values. Mr. Harris did not inscribe his values in marble; he lived them for all to see. The same holds true for any CEO building a value-based Culture. You must be prepared to live your values at all times.

FROM ARTICULATION TO PRACTICE

In 2005, Andy Roddick—at that time one of the top tennis players in the world—was playing Fernando Verdasco of Spain at the Rome Masters tournament in Rome. Roddick was the number one seed and a heavy favorite to win the match. He was at the top of his game.

With Roddick on the verge of a triple match point, the linesman called Verdasco's second serve out and awarded

Roddick the match. Roddick knew, however, that the serve had not been out, but had hit on the line. He could have remained mute and accepted the victory. Instead, he showed the umpire the mark on the clay where the ball had hit. The umpire reversed the call and awarded the point to Verdasco. Verdasco made the most of his second chance coming all the way back to win the match and eliminate Roddick from the tournament.

Sportswriters estimate that Roddick's honesty not only cost him the match but also impacted his international ranking and, of course, cost him a large purse of prize money. For Roddick, his integrity as a player was tied up in how the game should be played. He believed that players owed it to one another to manage the game fairly and accurately. His values were more important than the outcome of a game, or even a career.

The Beat writer William S. Burroughs once said, "The aim of education is the knowledge, not of facts, but of values." It is not enough for a CEO to simply take inventory of organizational values. Those values must then be translated into accessible statements that convey what actions are required to fulfill them.

Human behavior is acutely sensitive to and influenced by physical and emotional environmental factors. Mr. Harris's story illustrates this point, and you will start to see the same kinds of stories developing in your business. In his bestselling book *The Tipping Point*, Malcom Gladwell explains that even biological "epidemics are sensitive to the conditions and circumstances of the times and places in which they occur."

With this in mind, how do we introduce our values to the team in a way that ensures they take hold and work on the subconscious level to produce the behaviors we want to see? How do we create an epidemic of enthusiasm for the Culture we are building?

Now that you have a set of finely crafted value statements, anchored by a contextual framework tailored to the unique cultural identity of your organization, you must now let the stories behind each of those values come out. By finding the stories and using them to anchor rituals that emphasize the importance of your Culture, you'll unleash a wave of creativity and focus in your company. Ritual is the key. As Joseph Campbell famously said in his book *The Power of Myth*:

> A ritual is the enactment of a myth. And, by participating in the ritual, you are participating in the myth. And since myth is a projection of the depth wisdom of the psyche, by participating in a ritual, participating in the myth, you are being, as it were, put in accord with that wisdom, which is the wisdom that is inherent within you anyhow. Your consciousness is being reminded of the wisdom of your own life.

Let's take the next step in the process of building your Culture.

RITUAL EFFORT

"Ritual consists of the external practices of spirituality that help us become more receptive and aware of the closeness of our lives to the sacred. Ritual is the act of sanctifying action—even ordinary action—so that it has meaning. I can light a candle because I need the light or because the candle represents the light I need."

—CHRISTINA BALDWIN

They stand before you, fearless and defiant, a line of men large and heavily muscled. One of them yells and the rest join him in a rhythmic chant as the line slowly advances, each man stomping his feet and bending to a wide-legged squat. To demonstrate their disdain, they grunt and slap their chests with the palms of their hands as they continue to advance. This is the challenge of the haka—the ritual war dance of the Maori, the indigenous People of New Zealand.

The Haka was originally performed by warriors before a battle to intimidate the opposition with their martial prowess. Today, the New Zealand national rugby team, the All Blacks, perform a chilling rendition of the haka before each match. Their performance has made the war dance known throughout the world.

Although it is primarily associated with men preparing for war, haka are also performed by women and permeate all parts of Maori Culture. There are haka to welcome guests, acknowledge achievements, or to celebrate marriages and funerals. The different parts of the body—hands, arms, legs, feet, voice, eyes, tongue—can be used to express whatever feelings are relevant to the occasion. For the Maori, the haka is a ritual that shapes and defines their Culture. Not simply about war, it holistically celebrates Maori history and life.

Virtually every country around the globe has one or more rituals emblematic of its Culture. Each summer, thousands of People on horseback ride to southern Spain, a celebration of Pentecost called the Pilgrimage of El Rocío. In India, residents of the town of Varanasi perform the Ganga Aarti ceremony to honor the Ganges River. People from across the country make a pilgrimage to the ceremony at least once in their lifetime. In Sweden, girls dance around the maypole on Midsummer Eve—believed to be a magical time for love.

COMMUNAL IDENTITY

Rituals are the outward manifestation of our inner lives. They define our origins and our aspirations; not only who we are, but who we wish to become. They support our values and give us purpose and structure. They provide us with an identity within our communities. Without them, we lose our sense of connection.

By packaging a specific aspect of Culture into a ritual, you make that aspect easier to share and transmit, with repetition conditioning members of the community to think and behave in ways that align with the Culture. That's a very anthropological way of saying that practice makes perfect, and we all know that reinforcement is useful. Rituals are part of what makes us human, and for this very reason they are an everyday part of our lives.

For the religious among us, the act of going to church, synagogue, mosque, or other place of worship each week is a cultural ritual. We repeat it at regular intervals with a specific group of People. The services at our church of choice likely follow a regular format, and the contents of that ritual—from singing hymns or chanting scripture to praying collectively— are designed to uphold and strengthen the values of that group, and to reinforce our identity as members of the tribe. Group values likely range from the spiritual to the communal, and over time, the expression of those values begins to attract People to the group who share similar ideas and can then participate in the rituals. The act of creating and practicing rituals can transform an aspiration into a realized value. Link a series of these rituals together, and you begin to transform your Culture.

As we've seen, the Ritz-Carlton's Daily Line-Up is an opportunity to review and reaffirm the company's values—a daily ritual. The interaction lasts only a few minutes, but that's enough to bring the values back to the forefront of everyone's minds, indelibly reinforcing the message: "These are our values and today is a new opportunity to practice them."

In my own company, we highlight a weekly Be Attitude by turning the spotlight on a person who embodied that Be Attitude. We use our Be Attitudes to start meetings, and as I mentioned earlier, we actively use them in our decision-making process. If a choice does not embody multiple Be Attitudes, that's a sign that it does not align with our values and is, therefore, not fit for our attention.

We live our values. That's what every powerful business Culture does as well. From Zappos to Google to Apple, the whole of a company and all of its People are immersed in the values of the Culture. When those values are practiced across the company, amazing things happen for the business because everyone serves the same mission with their unique strengths.

Rituals are the route to practice. If you do not build rituals, your business will be just another venture where the values are on the website but nobody—not you and certainly not your employees—takes them seriously, and that will be most evident in the company's performance. Ritual is the path to preventing such a result.

BUILDING RITUALS

Rituals come in all shapes and sizes, and each variation is important in its own way. If you are a sports fan, you can likely identify the range of rituals that go into dedicating yourself to a team. Small rituals, like wearing a jersey to work on game days require a relatively low amount of effort—after all, you just have to put on a shirt. Regularly hosting friends and family for season games takes more work. You clean and decorate the house. You prepare a table full of snacks and appetizers. You watch all of the pre- and postgame coverage.

A variety of rituals come together to form the Culture of what it means to be a fan of a sports team. Many of these rituals feel organic, but if you look closely, sports marketing and branding companies painstakingly nurture and promote the behaviors that strengthen engagement with the team brand. In this way, they use rituals to strengthen the community around their product—a team. Think of the "Terrible Towel" of the Pittsburgh Steelers, or the "Tomahawk Chop" of the Atlanta Braves. Neither of these appeared on the scene organically. Rather, the teams actively promoted these rituals.

Still don't think rituals hold sway over our beliefs? Tennis legend Serena Williams doesn't change her socks for the duration of an entire tournament—162 matches—because early in her career, as she was poised to claim a great tournament victory, she changed into a fresh pair of socks, played miserably, and lost the title. Do smelly socks have some mystical power over her playing ability? Of course not, but her ritual centers her focus, reinforces her beliefs, and gives her a mental edge.

What rituals are currently in place in your business? How does your organization informally introduce its Culture to new People joining the company? How do you celebrate transitions from one job to the next? What actions do you collectively take to express gratitude to individual contributors on the team? Each of these is a ritual, repeated in anthropological shorthand to underline those things we find important.

In some ways, a ritual that sprouts up organically among your People can be a sign of a healthy Culture, but if you presently have a least-common-denominator Culture, it's likely that you are dealing with least-common-denominator rituals. Maybe your sales team meets every Thursday for a drink and to complain about the direction of the company.

Or maybe your software development team plays darts in the break room after a successful release because they feel a sense of camaraderie and family.

You probably have more rituals in place than you realize, but be honest with yourself: do they represent the values you believe are important to your business? For a ritual to be a positive force in your business, it should have the following ingredients:

1. Rituals carry a purpose. Each ritual should have as its purpose the introduction or reinforcement of a shared value. There are activities that groups of People do that do not rise to the level of ritual. It is purpose that differentiates a routine activity and a ritual.

2. Rituals repeat. Rituals are meant to happen over and over again. While some fringe aspects of the ritual may change, its core stays the same and is easily repeated. The frequency of repetition can vary from ritual to ritual, but they should reoccur with some regularity. Every time they reoccur, they must convey the same message in order to reinforce a core belief.

3. Rituals are practical. For rituals to be effective, they must be accessible and easy for your People to practice. If the action is too complex or burdensome, the likelihood of regular ritual practice drops significantly.

The Ritz-Carlton's Daily Line-Up satisfies each of these elements. The meeting re-emphasizes company values, happens each day, and is brief enough to be accessible to everyone. Michael, a doorman at the Ritz-Carlton in Atlanta, was asked if it becomes boring, talking about the same things each day. He responded, "I can honestly say there hasn't been a single day that I haven't learned something at the Line-Up. You get to know your teammates, how they think about things. You learn about the company you work for. You get to share something about yourself too. Maybe it makes me a better team member—I'm sure it does—but it definitely makes me a better person."

In my own business, each week we have a Be Attitude of the Week to focus on. Every Monday morning, everyone gets an email from someone in the company highlighting that week's Be Attitude. The email shares a story of how that person witnessed the Be Attitude being practiced at our company. It also includes some commentary on why it is important to them. We do it fifty-two weeks a year, which means that each of our thirteen value statements is center stage in these emails four times a year.

INTRODUCING RITUAL CHANGE

When a farmer sets out to revive a depleted field, he spends years rotating through the right kinds of crops, adding the right fertilizers, all the while testing and retesting the soil content to measure its progress. Changing the course of your company may not take a decade, but you should plan for the transformation to be gradual. You may encounter resistance to a new ritual, especially if your existing Culture is somewhat toxic, so you will need to convince your internal leaders to champion the new initiative.

Once you see the first round of rituals taking root, you can begin to add a new layer of rituals, and then another, building to the point where your Culture automatically expresses itself through rituals. Eventually, you will reach a time when you no longer need to add new rituals and can instead focus on the health of the rituals you have in place.

THE SHAPES OF RITUALS

The size and frequency of rituals vary with their reason for being practiced. As the architect of the Culture, you have to strike a balance with your company's daily rituals. If you have too many, you will overrun your People with tasks and miss out on opportunities to build and celebrate your Culture on special occasions. Likewise, if you rely only on big, infrequent events, your Culture will lack the reinforcement it needs to remain strong. Balance is necessary.

The amount of effort it takes to practice a ritual is typically tied to its frequency. Rituals that happen multiple times in a day are small and lightweight. As you move up the scale toward an annual company-wide ritual, you will likely see that much more effort becomes necessary. Let's look at the different kinds of rituals and explore examples of each:

1. Persistent Rituals are constantly practiced. For example, organizations like the Ritz-Carlton and Chick-fil-A train their teams to say "My pleasure" instead of "You're welcome" when customers thank them. This sets the tone for both customers and employees. Small actions taken on an as-needed basis serve to reinforce the Culture and can make a big impact over time.

2. Daily Rituals are lightweight reminders that serve to set the tone for the work to be completed that day. Software developers who practice an agile programming methodology value incremental progress and firm launch dates. At software companies, members of the programming team attend a daily "stand-up" meeting to quickly cover the progress made on team-owned tasks. Each person sets his daily workload based on the feedback from the team as a whole so that deadlines are met and work rhythms respected.

3. Weekly Rituals usually follow a regular schedule and may require preparation time from at least one employee. For example, the weekly email that we use in my own firm is a relatively easy ritual for the majority of the company to participate in. Employees quickly read the email, then take a few moments to respond and comment via our Slack channel, typically congratulating the individual praised in the email. For the person writing the email,

which we rotate weekly, it takes thought and care, but by spreading the responsibility, we keep it from becoming a chore for any one person or team. Weekly rituals come in other variations. Casual Friday is technically a weekly ritual, but on its own, it is not very interesting. A Casual Friday that is used to fundraise for a cause—donate a dollar to the local homeless shelter and you get to wear jeans—makes the ritual more meaningful. Get creative and remain thoughtful.

4. Monthly Rituals are generally events lasting an hour or more and requiring preparation and active participation from employees. For example, some businesses use regular town hall meetings to give employees an opportunity to voice concerns and receive updates from management. Other companies allow employees to spearhead committees on charity initiatives, and those groups often connect monthly. Your own business might offer optional employee education, such as bonus training and workshops that are enriching for everyone involved.

5. Annual Rituals are typically landmark moments for the business that occupy the attention of the entire company. Many businesses participate in annual retreats or communally celebrate holidays. These events are opportunities to ritually revisit your values. Timberland, for example, offers a "Path of Service" initiative where their employees can dedicate forty hours of paid time off to serving their communities and can apply to spend as much as six months on paid sabbatical to effect positive

change. Timberland puts value-based guiderails on what projects qualify and has used this program as a recruiting tool to great success.

I hope that you are beginning to see the full potential of a forceful Culture. Many businesses just pay lip service to their Culture. Don't do that. Make your values come alive in a creative and impactful way that demonstrates to your People and to the world what your company represents.

MONITORING AND NURTURING

As you deploy the rituals you have identified within your business, you will need an effective way to track and measure their impact so that you can ensure their success. If you kick off a ritual that doesn't land—People have no interest in it and are only going through the motions—kill it. There is nothing more corrosive than a forced and inauthentic ritual. It harms the Culture and diminishes your People's respect for the company.

If you don't regularly assess your Culture, your company can begin to drift. The farther out you drift, the more resources you'll need to correct the problem and the more likely you'll be to lose your moorings. To prevent this, make a plan to improve your Culture that outlines a phased approach and then track your progress as you begin to take action.

Implementing cultural change is no different from any other

project in your workplace. Culture is an internal initiative that should be treated with the same care and attention as a new company website or the next version of your core product offering. Lay out roadmaps. Assign tasks. Convene regularly to assess progress with the relevant team leaders and managers.

Rituals are outward manifestations of the values and beliefs that define your Culture. But what does a well-functioning, ritualized Culture look like?

One of the senior team members in my firm unexpectedly became his mother's caregiver when she was diagnosed with a rare neurological condition. Pick's disease, as it's known, attacks a patient's brain by shrinking its frontal lobe. The frontal lobe governs language, reasoning, risk management, and a host of other important social relationship functions. To be a caregiver to a Pick's patient is a heavy burden; you watch your loved one revert through each of life's phases. At my company, we love this team member, and it was hard to see him deal with the challenges that beset his mother.

Two years after the diagnosis, I was consulting with an out-of-state client, and I received the news that his mother had passed away. I canceled the rest of my meetings with the client, booked a flight to Orlando, and called my friend to offer my condolences. He appreciated the gesture and asked if I might sit with his family at the funeral. While I was away, the office manager broke the news to the office and shared the address of the church so that our team members could send flowers if they wished.

At the service, I sat up front in the large Catholic church with my friend and his family. My friend was to deliver the eulogy, and the priest invited him to address those in attendance. When he ascended the pulpit and looked out over the audience, he choked up and had to take a minute to compose himself. The priest took over to give him time to collect himself, and then my friend delivered a beautiful eulogy, a tender and heartrending message of love for his mom, which began, "Most men only know their mothers as an adult, but because of Pick's disease, I knew mine as a child too."—There was not a dry eye in the building. Even the priest shed a tear over such an expression of love.

After my friend sat down, he leaned over to me and whispered to me that he was embarrassed. I whispered back, "Why? It's your mom's funeral, everyone understands." He shook his head briskly and said, "That's not why," as he hooked his thumb over his shoulder indicating that I should look behind me.

Our entire firm was behind me, from the receptionist to senior vice presidents. No one there lived within three hours of the church, but with no direction from me, they had arranged to shut the business down for the day and made the trip. They had come to provide their support because at our company, we believe that no one should have to go through an experience like a parent's funeral alone.

That's how Culture shows up in the behaviors of your People. I devote myself to making our Culture persistent, durable, and impactful to the People we are blessed to call our own.

SECTION III

—

PEOPLE

UNDERSTANDING PEOPLE

"It is good people who make good places."

—ANNA SEWELL

Understanding People is hard. People are bundles of walking contradictions, confusions, and irrationality. We're wired to be self-preserving, which can make us come off as selfish, egotistical, and greedy. And yet we also practice the virtue of living with others to reap the personal and professional benefits of being part of a community. Only by connecting with other People are we able to achieve our full potential. The trick is recognizing and joining with the right People.

PICKING THE RIGHT PEOPLE

One of your tasks as the CEO is to pick the right People to

power your business. Building an environment in which they can thrive—your Culture—is critical. But a Culture without its People properly aligned and focused is an oxymoron. Culture cannot exist without People, and People must be properly aligned with the Culture for results to manifest.

Building a Culture of like-minded People is inherent in the CEO's role, and it is as much an art as a science. Hire the wrong person—morale crumbles and performance suffers. Bring on the right talent—performance increases and growth accelerates. Once the right People are onboard, they grow and change, engage with new challenges, and embrace the lessons of success and failure. This growth, while positive, can pose its own set of challenges.

CEOs know that finding the right mix of skills, knowledge, experience, and cultural fit can be a Herculean task, but that job belongs to the CEO and no one else. While you may delegate specific tasks in the hiring process and involve those who will work day-to-day with the new hire, as the CEO you must make the ultimate decision to introduce a new person into a carefully constructed cultural ecosystem.

Google's co-founder and former CEO Larry Page famously approved or rejected every one of the company's hires—over 6,500 People in 2017. When asked why, he explained: "It helps me to know what's really going on." Google employs over eighty-five thousand People on six continents, and its CEO still played a personal role in each hire.

Richard Fairbank, the CEO of Capital One, has more than fifty thousand employees. Regarding those employees, he noted that, "At most companies, People spend two percent of their time recruiting and seventy-five percent managing their recruiting mistakes." If hiring is important enough to be a part of the daily routines of Richard Fairbank, Larry Page, and a host of other CEOs, shouldn't it be part of yours?

Think about it this way: we might reduce a company to the formula: Company = People x Culture x Focus. To increase the value of the company, we must increase each of those three parts. That said, People matter more than any other variable, and there is no area where a CEO's impact will be more directly and widely felt.

Some CEOs may complain that recruiting takes up too much time that could be invested in other activities. They might suggest that People lower down in the organization are better equipped to know the skills necessary for a specific position. While not wholly incorrect, these sentiments betray a lack of nuance in understanding of the CEO's role. A company's hiring managers have different motivations from its CEO. While both want to fill positions with People who can do the job, only the CEO, as steward of the Culture, can make the tough choices about hiring those who best align with it.

THE THREE DIMENSIONS

A CEO who understands People—how they tick, what they need in order to function and achieve—has a sustainable competitive advantage few others can rival. In a previous chapter, we introduced a mental model of the Three Dimensions: "I Think," "I Feel," "I Am." That same model is useful when applied to understanding your current employees and potential hires. By leveraging this framework, we can construct an effective hiring and management process rooted in a deep understanding of yourself, the business, and the People who will join the team.

Buried within each person's emotional composition is a deeply seated, individual belief system. This belief system is called the "self-image," a phrase coined by Dr. Maxwell Maltz in his classic book *Psycho-Cybernetics*. It controls a person's actions, feelings, behaviors, and abilities. As discussed earlier, Ron Willingham spent his career exploring the implications of the self-image and has articulated that each person is made up of three separate yet interrelated dimensions.

THE "I THINK" DIMENSION

The intellectual dimension is the rational, conscious, cognitive part of us that learns information, remembers facts and figures, and coldly analyzes data. It's the perceiving part of us that takes in and assigns meaning to stimuli and input. Our formal education is directed at this intellectual part of us, as we are taught to remember the names of kings and the battles they won, the atomic weight of hydrogen, the quadratic formula, or the Spanish word for "library." For decades, the education system focused solely on the "I Think" dimension of human behavior, and a student's potential success was measured with a quantified score known as IQ, or the intelligence quotient.

In recruiting, we must pay attention to a candidate's intellectual abilities. How they resaon, their cognitive limitations, what they know, and how quickly they learn are items to be assessed in forming a full opinion of someone who may be joining the company. Most companies, however, only focus on this aspect of the potential hire and look no deeper. That's a mistake. Is the most intelligent person in your business always the most successful?

We all know that there is more to us than just our thinking parts. People aren't robots or computers. We are complex creatures, and yet many hiring and management processes do not go beyond the "I Think" dimension. They only assess a person's skills and ability to competently perform the tasks required for the position. Barring any glaring red flags in the candidate's stability, a job offer is made. There are dimensions in us that are not touched by knowledge, education, reason, or functional logic, and those dimensions affect the performance of the People you bring into your business as much as their intellectual abilities. Any system that ignores that truth is doomed to failure.

THE "I FEEL" DIMENSION

This is the part of us that senses our feelings and produces our emotions. Emotions fuel our actions, giving animation to behaviors. In battles between our intellectual and emotional dimensions, our emotions carry the day 85 percent of the time. If we limit our work as CEOs to evaluating the "I Think" dimensions of our People, we ignore the majority of what makes them thrive.

Many businesses intentionally ignore the "I Feel" dimension because emotions are not considered professional, as if People could check their emotions at the door and show up for work with only their intellectual faculties. While it's true that emotions can be volatile and pose a challenge when they go unchecked, we must also recognize that the fire emotion brings to our everyday choices makes us uniquely human. Emotions in the workplace should not be ignored. When nurtured and coached, employees use their emotions to provide creativity, passion, and engagement.

In the 1960s, social scientists became cognizant of the

power of emotions. Over the subsequent decades, research has revealed that our emotions are present in every human interaction. Presented with this evidence, HR departments started to focus on useful concepts such as "self-esteem" and "emotional resilience" in evaluating potential candidates for an open position.

In 1995, Daniel Goleman's influential book *Emotional Intelligence* asserted that it is not cognitive intelligence but rather emotional intelligence that guarantees success in life and business. Goleman went so far as to suggest a measurement tool that could quantify a person's emotional intelligence. Similar to IQ tests for intellectual prowess, we can now measure a person's emotional intelligence with an EQ score. While neither IQ nor EQ should be the overriding factor when considering a new hire, a wise CEO looks at both in assessing a candidate's personality.

THE "I AM" DIMENSION

Almost as soon as the idea of emotional intelligence became commonplace, academics and social scientists began to question whether there was something deeper than emotions that could be the true source of behaviors. Do emotions have a wellspring from which they arise? We now know that they do.

The third dimension of human behavior, the "I Am" dimension, is sometimes called the Creative Unconscious. In this dimension, we house our values, self-image, beliefs, and sense of right and wrong. This is where you keep the things that make you uniquely you. If you were to change one of these things, you would no longer be the same person.

Hardwired into our "I Am" dimension is our sense of purpose, a distillation of what we believe about the world and how we fit into it. When our purpose is clear, we find tremendous amounts of mental energy. When it is murky, or when our daily activities no longer connect to it, we can choke out that flow of energy. When that happens, burnout, depression, and a host of other psychological maladies begin to appear.

When you are able to hire, manage, and lead in a way that silently communicates with People's "I Am" dimensions, your life will be vastly different from what it is today. No longer will you have to drag People along on the mission-path with you, cajoling reluctant employees to do better work, motivating them to meet your expectations, begging them to produce results. Instead, you will be surrounded by a team that shares your values. By having your team own the individual tasks you assign, you will free yourself to focus on your most important work.

WHY DO WE CARE?

Besides being interesting on a purely academic level, why is any of this important to us as CEOs? If we want to get the most from our People—the most productivity, the highest results, the best quality—then we must manage them from a whole-person perspective. You would never think of hiring a new employee and neglecting to teach them the important details about your product or service. Similarly, you should never complete a new hire orientation and say to those assembled, "Your feelings are unimportant and have no place here. Never mention them during work hours again," but how many of us make a conscious commitment to connecting with our People at the "I Am" level?

When we come to our People with an awareness that they experience the world in three different but complementary ways, we unleash torrents of creative energy that elevate the meaning of our work. Working ceases to be work by any traditional definition and becomes a spiritual experience. What CEO wouldn't want to achieve that state of being for themselves and those around them?

THE "NEXT LEVEL"

Every leader has, at some point, expressed a desire to "take it to the next level": to elevate the quality of their organization's work, output, and results. Entrepreneurs, CEOs, business owners of all stripes—we all want our organizations to function with less friction and more reward for the work invested. Because organizations are simply entities that exist to unify the actions of People, it stands to reason that to "level up" our organizations, we have to "level up" our People. But do People have levels?

ELLIOT JAQUES AND LEVELS OF WORK

Renowned organizational psychologist Elliot Jaques spent his career proving that every person has a zone of time in which they have the highest output of the best work without supervision. People have "time horizons," and People's positions have "levels of work." Matching a person's time horizon to a position with a corresponding level of work is the end goal of management, according to Jaques.

Jaques was a Canadian-born psychologist, professor, and business ethicist who developed the concept of corporate Culture, coined the term "midlife crisis," and helped found the internationally acclaimed Tavistock Institute of Human Relations. He worked with the largest organizations in the world from national militaries to multinational corporations. In a career spanning more than six decades, he worked ceaselessly to answer the question: "Why is it that two People, similarly situated, can perform so differently in the same position?" His answer: time horizons and levels of work.

Jaques believed that organizations should be arranged hierarchically on the basis of levels of work. Those team members with the ability to think, plan, and execute over a longer period of time without direct supervision should be in senior positions and supported by those with shorter individual time horizons. In an era when "flat" org-charts, titleless jobs, and team-led companies are all the rage, Jaques's philosophy flies in the face of conventional wisdom. To put Jaques's philosophy into a model we can use might look something like this:

LEVEL	FUNCTION	HORIZON	FOCUS	TOOLS	THOUGHTS	TITLE
5	Lead the Company	Two to Ten Years	Vision	Writing	Intuition/ Theory	CEO
4	Manage the Systems	Quarterly to Annually	Mission	Database	Conceptual/ Models	VP
3	Manage the Processes	Monthly to Quarterly	Strategy	Spreadsheet	Ideational/ Concrete	Manager
2	Supervise the Work	Weekly to Monthly	Tactics	Calendar	Imaginal/ Concrete	Supervisor
1	Do the Work	Daily to Weekly	Product	Physical Tools	Perceptual/ Concrete	Worker

In Jaques's world, every organization struggles with the issue of having its People tasked at the wrong level. In fact, his research suggested that as many as 65 percent of People were in the wrong position. This is frustrating for the both the employee and the employer and is the genesis of "burnout," another term coined by Jaques. Preventing burnout by designing positions according to the level of work required, then filling them with People whose time horizons were a perfect fit, was not just good business for Jaques, it was a moral act. CEOs who understand Jaques and his philosophy have a competitive advantage over those who simply hire

People for their personalities and experience and hope for the best.

Consider this: Michael Jordan is a legendary basketball player but had a mediocre professional baseball career. If his athletic career were judged solely on his baseball ability, it would be forgettable. That's ridiculous, of course, because even nonbasketball fans know that Jordan was a basketball icon. Even today, kids who never saw him play for the Chicago Bulls wear his jersey.

In your company today, or perhaps in the round of interviews you have scheduled next week, you could have a Michael Jordan in your midst—but he or she might be playing the wrong sport. When we ignore levels of work, we may unknowingly leave an all-star on the bench.

Put another way, you wouldn't ask your receptionist to fill in for twelve weeks while your Vice President of Manufacturing is out on maternity leave. Not only would she be ill-prepared for the job, she would also need constant feedback, evaluation, and assurance—all of which would take away productive time from another employee without improving her skillset. In the end, she would fail, and such failure would have a lasting impact on her "I Am" dimension. Jaques would place the blame for this squarely on the CEO's shoulders.

The converse is also true. Suppose you take the VP and have

her answer the phones and greet clients for twelve weeks. Yes, she could figure out the mechanics of the position, but how long would it take for her to become bored and start to unnecessarily re-engineer aspects of the job? How much strife and aggravation would this create?

Think about it. If Jaques is right and over half of your team members could be in the wrong roles, how much success are you leaving on the table every year? If you have even 25 percent of your Michael Jordans playing baseball, that's a tragedy in terms of their individual potential and the potential of your business. Jaques consulted with private companies large and small, as well as with the United States military and international charities. All of his research supported this conclusion: People are happier and more productive in roles that fit their time horizons.

The power of understanding this model cannot be overstated. As CEOs who want to do the right thing for our People by helping them maximize their creative output in pursuit of shared corporate goals, this model stands as one of the most important we can use.

When we assign a person the wrong role, regardless of whether we move them "up" or "down" in terms of complexity or responsibility, we sow the seeds of discord and discontent, and we hurt our People. If we make enough of these missteps, company morale begins to falter and our Culture suffers.

Using this model to our advantage improves the Culture, our People, and ultimately the Numbers they produce.

APPLYING THE MODEL

As you study Jaques's model, you will begin to place your People into one of the strata identified. This is natural and necessary. Simply knowing the levels of your team members, though, is only half the work. You must also place each position—independent of the person who currently staffs it—within the framework.

Getting time horizons and levels right is a masterstroke of leadership. It requires you to complete two tasks: a position classification and a People inventory. To complete your position classification, take a long look at each position on your organizational chart. Ask yourself: "What is the ideal amount of time that a person in this position should be able to work without direct supervision or guidance to produce optimal results?" You may phrase the answer within a time horizon such as "Weekly to Monthly," "Monthly to Quarterly," or "Annually."

Complete your People inventory by examining each person in your organization with an eye toward their personal time horizon. Ask yourself: "How long can this person work without direct supervision and still produce optimal results?" Your answer should fall within a narrow horizon such as "Quarterly to Annually" or "Monthly to Quarterly."

Once you have completed both exercises, compare the results. What conclusions can you reach? Do you have People in your organization who are ill-suited to the position they're in?

RESTRUCTURING LEVELS AND TIME HORIZONS

Several years ago, my organization reached a crossroads and we had to make a bold decision. Our sales had been increasing, and it was becoming too great a burden for a salesperson to generate a new client and service their reasonable needs throughout our client lifecycle. We needed to create some role specialization—we needed to create a Client Success team.

It was a challenge. We had an institutional belief that our salespeople were honor-bound to service the clients they onboarded. Not having them do so seemed wrong and out of step with our "Client First" Culture. Compounding the problem, we didn't have anyone on our team with specialized knowledge of how a Client Success team functioned; we had always just figured out what was necessary to make our clients happy. It was an undisciplined, unprofitable approach.

Earlier in the year, we had added a new sales team member named Robert. His first year was adequate, but his results weren't impressing anyone. His job was Level One—sell and service clients. At the end of the year we spoke, and he shared his frustrations with me. In that conversation, he let me know that he would be leaving the organization at the end of the year. In the course of our discussions, I listened closely to the language he used to describe his work and it became apparent that while he was tasked as a Level One, he operated on a Level Three time frame. I had offered him the wrong position.

Over the following weeks, I shared with him my vision of revamping our sales and service organizations. I asked him to be a founding member of the Client Success team and help me build that team out as its Director, a Level Three position. We threw his old compensation plan out and made a new one commensurate with the needs of the new position. His work in the new position has been nothing short of life-altering for me, my organization, and our salespeople. It has allowed us to more efficiently onboard new clients and to keep them happy long-term. If I hadn't known the Jaques model, I would have lost him forever and he would have left the role thinking less of himself.

As you can see, applying Jaques's ideas at an organizational level can dramatically influence success. To experience that success, however, you must look at People as individuals by applying the idea of levels and time horizons to each person. When you understand the three ideas we covered in this chapter—the Three Dimensions, levels of work, and time horizons—you will transform your approach to hiring, staffing, and managing in a way that brings out the best in your People. Here is where your insight into your People becomes a powerful driver of your company's success. When you recognize that each person operates within the dimensions of "I Think," "I Feel," and "I Am" and marry that idea with an understanding of each person's abilities, you unlock a uniquely effective hiring and management tool. While other CEOs guess at what People need and where they might fit in—or just manage People with a one-size-fits-all system— you have a proven framework for engaging and leading.

THE TALENT ACQUISITION MINDSET

"I am convinced that nothing we do is more important than hiring and developing people. At the end of the day you bet on people, not on strategies."

—LAWRENCE BOSSIDY, GE

Great CEOs recognize that hiring the right People is essential to the success of their business. How essential? The 2019 CEO Benchmarking Report reveals that finding the right talent has become the C-Suite's top priority. Nearly 70 percent of CEOs say they need help with talent-related strategies. Key challenges include holding employees accountable, getting the maximum performance out of People, and creating a positive work environment.

Why is talent so important? A *Harvard Business Review* study reports that high performers typically produce 400 percent higher results than average performers. The gap only widens as jobs become more complex. In fields such as software development, high performers are an amazing eight times more productive.[5] Management guru Jim Collins sums it up best: "The single biggest constraint on the success of my organization is the ability to get and to hang on to enough of the right people."

Though we may recognize the critical role talent plays in an organization, we often lack the tools and processes needed to best understand the People we want to hire and the positions they ultimately fill. With the framework we established in the Three Dimensions, the levels of work, and time frames, we can build a hiring process that succeeds.

By that, I mean that you can bring People into roles in which they can thrive personally and professionally. This is the ever-elusive "fit" that CEOs so often pursue but cannot consistently describe or achieve. When you hire the right People for the right positions, performance goes up, morale improves, and employee churn goes down. Yes, you have heard this promise before, but the approach we are about to discuss is not only field-proven, it is built on what drives People in their "I Am" dimensions.

---

5   Karie Willyerd, "What High Performers Want at Work," *Harvard Business Review*, November 18, 2014, https://hbr.org/2014/11/what-high-performers-want-at-work.

CEOs don't hire People to fill jobs. CEOs recruit talent to grow the company. They understand that there is an inverse relationship between the control exerted by an executive and the proper functioning of a team. Control stifles creativity; creativity leads to growth and performance.

To make success a reality, we must shift our mindsets away from filling jobs and adopt a vision long prevalent in the entertainment industry: talent management. In any given year, scores of films, Broadway shows, books, television shows, and other works of media are produced around the world. The one common denominator that separates the truly memorable—and thus, monetizable—from the rest is talent.

Webster's defines talent as our "natural gifts in the form of an innate calling or aptitude for a particular skill or task." Talent is inborn—it's what we're effortlessly good at. Talent can also be developed through repeated practice and the expansion of our creative faculties.

The best CEOs see their People as one-of-a-kind performers with innate gifts that deliver business results. Talent acquisition is an art, but one that can be taught. It produces a seismic shift in how organizations select their members and its effect is cumulative: talent attracts talent.

TALENT MANAGEMENT

The risks involved in making a Hollywood film have grown exponentially over the past two decades. To ensure a profit, film studios look for a sure thing—a tried-and-true story with a star who's a box-office draw. Occasionally it works. But usually it doesn't. Think of all the films you've seen where the casting was totally wrong. Not because the star had no talent but because they were just not the right "fit" for either the character they played or the film's storyline.

For Hollywood, choosing the right talent is critical. That's why the choice has to go beyond reputation or who a director likes to work with. The actor who gets the part should bring the script to life in a way no one else could have. If a movie's star isn't a good match, nothing can save it. The same holds true for the choices you make as a CEO—you can have the perfect script, the perfect setting, plenty of money, and a dynamite director, but if your talent isn't up to par, you're funding a flop. This is why we must look beyond résumés and reputations. Just as the actors a producer casts can make or break a film, the People you hire will have a lasting impact on the success of your company.

TALENT ACQUISITION

Finding candidates to fill positions is not hard. A recent study by Indeed.com revealed that the average position advertised has over forty-four applicants. If you asked your

HR department how many applications it sees for the average position, you might discover that hundreds of résumés are processed for any given opening. The challenge is to find the right person—the talent—who fits your Culture and will enhance the capabilities of the company. To do so, CEOs must throw out preconceived notions of "recruiting" and focus instead on "talent acquisition" strategies.

No Hollywood casting director would place a classified ad to cast a leading man in a blockbuster role. Instead, she seeks out relationships with People familiar with the style, work habits, and capabilities of potential performers to schedule auditions for the role. She isn't looking for someone who will do an adequate job; she is looking for the person can own the role as no one else can. Why should a CEO behave any differently?

Your answer might be that it is difficult to treat hiring with this same level of intensity given the sheer volume of positions you have to fill. If you are skeptical that you can personally impact long-term employee retention in today's job-hopping environment, remember that companies the size of Google still involve their key leaders in the talent acquisition process.

When you focus your work on the three things a CEO does and approach the task with a structured process, talent acquisition becomes much more achievable. To implement a talent acquisition philosophy, however, you have to leave behind some of the archaic ideas that persist around hiring. You have to adopt novel strategies to produce extraordinary results.

THE PROBLEM WITH PERSONALITY

There is a dirty little secret about most employers' recruiting processes: it's all about personality. If a process exists at all, it's designed to guarantee that the job goes to the most likable and sociable candidate, not the person who is the best fit for the position. Unconsciously, those doing the hiring ignore objective indicators of future performance, focus on personality, and end up hiring the candidate whose personality most closely matches their own.

Personality is an important part of our "I Am" dimension, but it is not predictive—ever—of job success. Even jobs that demand a high level of emotional intelligence, or EQ, can be done by People with different personality types. If personality were the answer—or even a part of the answer—then the personality tests that you've been running for years would mean that you have no recruiting or retention challenges in your business...but you do.

Which is why the CEO who is truly focused on talent acquisition rejects personality as a prime determinant and adopts a mindset and implements processes that select candidates based what we call the 4Cs: Culture, Capabilities, Compensation, and Commitment. The 4Cs represent the four stages of the interview process. At first glance, this approach may seem far more intense than anything you have used before. That is by design. We aren't just seeking someone to fill a role, we are seeking the only person who can own the role. We are looking for a star.

THE TALENT MINDSET

Customer retention is a prime objective of virtually every company. According to a study by Bain & Company, a mere 5 percent increase in customer retention can translate to a profit increase as high as 95 percent.[6] The same holds true for talent retention. Just as it is more profitable to keep your current customers, it is also more profitable to keep your current employees. The Center for American Progress found that replacing an employee costs roughly 21 percent of that employee's annual salary.[7] In other words, five bad hires equal an entire year of lost productivity. The time to focus on retaining your talent is when you hire them, not after they've been on board for a while.

Rethinking your talent acquisition process along the 4Cs

---

6   "Retaining customers is the real challenge," Bain & Company, January 20, 2006, https://www.bain.com/insights/retaining-customers-is-the-real-challenge/.

7   Heather Boushey, Sarah Jane Glynn, "There Are Significant Business Costs to Replacing Employees," Center for American Progress, November 16, 2012, https://www.americanprogress.org/issues/economy/reports/2012/11/16/44464/there-are-significant-business-costs-to-replacing-employees/.

model will get results. It is a novel approach, though, and there are some key points to review before adopting it. Like all things worth doing, this process requires some preparation to make sure it produces the results you want.

First, employers often wait too long to begin the recruiting process, which leads to timing pressure and poor hiring decisions. As much as it is within your control, you should begin hiring as soon as you recognize the need to do so. Sometimes this is before you've received notice from an incumbent or announced the departure of one. This means you must have the necessary collateral ready to go at a moment's notice. On your recruiting platform, you should have your job postings archived and ready to publish, and you should have your online profiling tools and interviewing resources available.

Second, the process is vastly different from most organization's current practices. A surprisingly large number of companies only interview candidates once before making an offer. In the 4Cs process, you are going to have at least four separate discussions with your candidates. Knowing this upfront prompts you to choose fewer People to meet and spend more time understanding them as potential team members.

Interviewers like being in charge, but in our approach, we put the candidate in control. Specifically, at the end of each interview, we send the candidate out with specific homework and the assignment to reestablish contact if, and only if, she feels an attachment to the company and a true desire for the position. You are teaching the candidate about accountability even from the first interview. You are eliminating those People who will accept a job but not pursue one—who are not engaged enough by the job to put in the work to land it.

Finally, we are fully transparent about the process, why it is different, and what we hope to gain by using it. We treat candidates like intelligent adults and don't keep secrets from them. Some interviewers get a perverse pleasure from keeping a candidate guessing and reaching for something she may never get—that isn't how you would want to be treated, and it isn't how you should treat others. In our process, we fully lay out the steps we are going to take, the why behind each step, and the expected timeline. Some candidates opt out immediately because they have no interest in our Culture or mission. We wish them well, then move on to more fruitful applicants. Still other candidates see the process for what it is, a risk-free way for them and the firm to investigate the things that really matter before making a decision that will impact the lives of many People.

Implementing the 4Cs is an enterprise-level commitment. Everyone in the organization must embrace it as critical to the mission. The more a CEO involves his People in the prime task of recruiting and selecting People, the more ownership they can take of the process and the result. When

People play a part in selecting new teammates, they psychologically feel obligated to ensure the success of those teammates once they are on board. The more you can make success a shared phenomenon, the better your recruiting and retention efforts will go.

THE TALENT ACQUISITION PROCESS

"Hire character. Train skill."

—PETER SCHUTZ

"I've never felt prouder to not receive a job offer," the card read. It was a thank-you card from a candidate who had interviewed for an open position with our firm. We had determined that while she was a great person with many strengths, our values and Culture weren't going to be a fit for her. We shared the news with her after the fourth interview, and I asked her if I could share her résumé with some other employers who were hiring. She agreed, and within two weeks she had a new job. "For the first time, I felt like someone in the working world was listening to me as a person, not just as an employee," the note finished. You can imagine my pride as I realized just how aligned our hiring process was with our values. Have you ever received a thank-you note from someone you didn't hire?

THE 4CS

So how did that note come about? As I said before, the 4Cs are Culture, Capabilities, Compensation, and Commitment. If a candidate isn't a fit in all four categories, he isn't a fit for the company. Each category has its own scheduled interview involving the CEO and other team members. Prior to the end of each interview, we decide whether to offer the candidate the opportunity to proceed with the process. If we do, we assign homework and a timeframe. If we don't, we very clearly state that we won't be proceeding and give a reason why. While some may find this difficult, I have had candidates tell me how much they appreciate the candor.

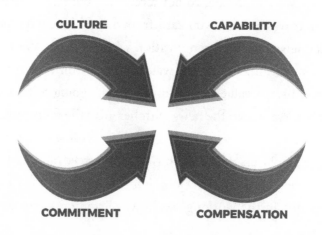

THE INTERVIEWS

For talent acquisition to be effective, the process needs to be structured, consistent, and repeatable. The process must also respect your time and be clearly measurable. Use the following outline for each of the interviews.

CULTURE

Culture is the cornerstone of the Talent Acquisition process. What does it profit a CEO who selects the most capable performer even if the candidate doesn't fit the Culture? Instead of enriching the organization, a bad cultural fit will harm the company by working against its values. Actively screening candidates for cultural fit means that the first interview is only about Culture, nothing else. In this interview, your task is to give the candidate a deep understanding of your organization's Culture so that he or she can judge for themselves whether or not the Culture is attractive. This may strike some CEOs as either counterintuitive or wrong. The approach, however, serves to communicate to the candidate just how central Culture is to your organization.

Introduce Your Culture

How do you best introduce and describe your Culture? The majority of CEOs with articulated Cultures will launch into a recitation of values statements and assertions of mission and focus. It's easy to do so. When you've spent time and energy doing Culture work, your enthusiasm for the work and its results will spill over into the conversation. Such enthusiasm is contagious but short-lived. It leaves the candidate with the knowledge that you are enthusiastic about the Culture, but it doesn't communicate why the candidate should be equally engaged in what you've created. We need a different approach.

One of the most effective techniques of argumentation taught by the ancient science of rhetoric is antithesis. Antithesis is a way of showing contrast between two desirable choices. Instead of sharing why a candidate should embrace your Culture and accept a job offer, we show the candidate why the position isn't a fit for everyone, only the right person. In short, we say, "Here are the four reasons you don't want to work here," and then frame those reasons in the context of the importance of Culture. This may seem like a gimmick, but it isn't. To select those who best belong, first show those who don't belong why they don't. The reasons you share this should echo the values you've articulated: "We have an integrity-based Culture, and those who aren't prepared to be graded in black and white find it a difficult environment to work in."

Telling the Story

Laying out a logical proposition isn't enough. People listen most attentively to stories. Author Erin Morgenstern speaks to the power of storytelling by saying, "You may tell a tale that takes up residence in someone's soul, becomes their blood and self and purpose. That tale will move them and drive them and who knows what they might do because of it, because of your words. That is your role, your gift." Storytelling is one of the most powerful tools we CEOs have at our disposal. It enables us to instantly illuminate for the listener our purpose, values, and Culture.

When searching for talent, we must provide the perfect story—the perfect context for answers to questions posed. Either the candidate sees himself in the story, or not. If he doesn't, he isn't a fit for the Culture. If he does, we move on to other parts of the interview and repeat the process.

If loyalty is one of the prized values of your organization, telling a story of a time when someone in your company demonstrated loyalty is more instructive than simply reading your value statement. It allows the candidate to ask herself privately, "Can I see myself doing that, or would I have acted differently?" It allows them to sample your Culture, to see if it feels right before making the decision to move in permanently. You should have a story for each of reason a candidate would not want to work for your company, and you should follow each of those stories with pointed questions.

For example, in my own cultural interviews, I tell the following story:

A couple of years ago, I published a sales bonus schedule allowing employees to earn points during the week and trade those points in for a bonus at the end of the year. People were naturally excited, but throughout the year, most did not hit their sales goals. At our all-hands meeting in January, a discussion ensued that boiled down to, "Where is our bonus money?"

Puzzled, I replied, "You did not hit your goals, so there is no bonus money." This triggered a great deal of hoopla about us not clearly establishing that bonuses were tied to goals, and there was not a unanimous consent as to what should happen next. After taking a day to think it through, I recognized that one of our Be Attitudes is to "Be Well-Spoken." I had a responsibility to own the impact of what I'd said. If I had not clearly identified the relationship between the bonuses and the goals, I had to honor my word to the team, which was hard because the year was soft for sales and our free cashflow was lacking.

I came back to the group and said, "I don't think I owe you these bonuses, but I also can't be the kind of man I want to be if I have this confusion attached to what I find important."

So, I issued the checks.

Almost immediately, seventy percent of the staff signed their checks and handed them back, acknowledging that they had not earned the bonuses. My actions made them rethink their own.

At the end of the ordeal, the thirty percent of the team who kept their checks were those who had reached their goals.

Would you have signed the check?

CALLING THE QUESTION

In Parliamentary procedure, there is a motion that can be made when a member of the body feels that all necessary points have been asserted and debated. The member then moves the Chair to "Call the Question," and put the resolution up for a final vote. It's time for conviction to prevail. No more fence-sitting or keeping your options open. Clarity cuts through the clutter and demands commitment: either "yay" or "nay."

In your talent acquisition process, the same clarity is necessary for both you and your candidate. "Are we going to go forward in our process, or is it time to call it quits?" Calling the Question and providing context on both the "yay" and "nay" answers will bring efficiency to your recruiting process. The faster you get to "nay" with candidates, the more time you free up for finding talent with the right cultural fit.

Poignant questions require reflection. I tell my candidates that I'm not as interested in their answers as they should be. They are answering the questions more for themselves than for me. If their answers align with my Culture, then they should opt to return for the next interview. If they don't, I wish them well, move on to the next candidate, and often forward their résumé to other employers. In this stage, your deliberate focus on Culture will help you to identify the individuals who aren't fits. The best candidates will typically reply within forty-eight hours. A timeline of a week or more suggests a great deal of hesitancy on their part, even if their ultimate answers align with your values.

You can expect to do most of the talking in this interview stage—about 80 percent of your time with the candidate will involve you telling stories and assigning homework. You can easily expect to lose as much as 25 percent of your candidate pool as People realize they don't fit the Culture you oversee—and that's a good thing for the long-term success of your company. Only those who value what we value are welcome in our Cultures. The interview process is your first opportunity to address that issue head-on.

CAPABILITIES

The first task of the Capabilities phase of the recruiting process is to give the candidate a comprehensive understanding of the open position. You should review in detail the job description, and explain what a typical day, week, and month look like for the position. Answer any and all questions about the job honestly and candidly. Involve others too. I always make time for my candidate to spend time with a recent hire and with a team member experienced in the position. I encourage questions like "What surprises have you found since being hired?" and "What do you wish you had known before taking the job?" Once those meetings have been held and the candidate is interested in moving forward, we dive deep into assessing how well she fits the job.

In preparing for the Cultural interview, you gathered stories that illustrated how your values are practiced in the course of daily life in your business. As we interview candidates to assess how capable they are of performing the tasks a certain position requires, we reach more for the concrete and objective. In this interview, we will ask the candidate to first understand the demands of the position, and then to prove that she is capable of filling those demands. Job fit, then, is measured in two ways:

1. The explicit measurement of hard skills by means of an objective assessment tool; and
2. Behavioral interviewing questions that assess a candidate's probable reaction to situations.

It's amazing to me how few CEOs assess concrete skills during the interview process. They take a candidate's word that she's mastered the day-to-day skills, when these skills are easily measurable. Depending on the skill to be measured, the assessment may be in person or it may be a written or electronic test taken outside of the office. Even if the candidate scores poorly—and is therefore not ideal for the position—I still recommend reviewing the results with her personally to help her understand why she isn't a fit. Though she may not end up being a part of your team, treating her with respect and demonstrating that she was not eliminated arbitrarily can help your reputation in the long run. You might also discover that the candidate is a fit for an entirely different position.

It's important to note here that we are looking only at objective assessments. So many organizations gratify their assessment urges with personality tests. Millions of dollars each year are spent assessing the personalities of People applying for jobs around the world. Personality tests were once offered as the panacea for all of our hiring woes, and yet after two decades of them being used in every industry imaginable, our hiring woes persist. The reason? Any personality type can do a given job depending on the circumstances. Personality has very little to do with job fit.

Following the objective assessment, begin to probe into relevant behavioral questions. Ask your candidates to share real-life examples of how they behaved under a general set of circumstances: "Can you share with me a time that you defused a situation involving an unhappy client?" or "Tell me about a time when the course of action that felt right to you ended up being wrong." Ideally, you should have three to five of these questions prepared so that you can get a well-rounded sense of how a person thinks and acts in the course of her work.

If we are satisfied with the assessment and the answers to our behavioral questions, and our candidate is interested after learning more about the open position, then we ask for three references. We review the list with the candidate and for each reference ask, "What will this person say about you?" and "What's a story I can ask this person about that will shed light on who you are at work?"

Then we call those references. It's stunning how few employers actually call a candidate's references. I always find out something about the candidate that is instructive to my recruiting process in these conversations.

At the conclusion of the capabilities stage, you should have the following:

- An understanding of the candidate's ability to meet performance requirements;
- An assessment of where the candidate's work level and time horizon rank;
- A sense of whether both of those factors are appropriate for the position—is there a job fit here?

As with the Culture interview, we send our candidate away for forty-eight hours to think about what they have learned about the position. If we like them for the job, and they are interested in learning more, we ask that they reach out to us to schedule the next interview. Another 25 percent of People will not make this next step, and that's okay because it suggests that they saw something in the position that they knew they didn't like. It's much better to know that early in the process, before we've introduced compensation into the discussion.

COMPENSATION

Is there anything more daunting than speaking candidly about compensation? We've been warned from our earliest days in business not to discuss compensation, and when the topic does arise it's usually accompanied by drama. This is unfortunate because compensation plays a central role in a candidate's decision-making process.

Yes, compensation can be an uncomfortable topic, and a significant portion of this discomfort stems from the reality that most CEOs lack an effective way to assess and discuss it. Traditionally, compensation rates have been based largely on an employer's subjective sense of market trends. This means paying what others are paying regardless of whether there is value to be created in a position or not.

This flies in the face of what we have come to understand about levels of work. Quite simply, a person's compensation should be based on the value that the person brings to the company. All positions are valuable in their own way, but a position that consumes more resources should create more value for the company.

This is such a core principle to our business that we share the philosophy during the interview process. In the cCompensation interview, we educate our candidates on how we compute value for dollars. By doing so, you show from the beginning that compensation is tied to a position's level of work. For the right hire, it is empowering—and sobering—to know that a portion of the value they create for the organization should be theirs to keep. Keep in mind, we are not looking for candidates who expect an orchard to produce fruit automatically because of the work of others. Rather, we empower candidates to find ways to improve the orchard, to plant more trees, and to bring a proactive approach and a real sense of ownership to their work.

After you have explained all this to the candidate, tell them the following: "We have spent a lot of time interviewing you for this position. If you think your capabilities match the job, we are interested in you coming back and telling us what compensation you think is fair."

That's right. You are asking the employee to tell you what they believe they are worth based on the whole of your conversation. This takes guts on your part: you're relinquishing control and changing your stance from "Here's my offer, take it or leave it" to "How much are you worth to my organization?" It's a tremendously revealing psychological exercise as well. Your candidate has to dig deep and decide for themselves what's really important to them in a well-rounded compensation package.

Give your candidate forty-eight hours to prepare their offer. Remind them to include the five elements of compensation: wage (salary or hourly depending on the position), vacation time, bonuses (annual or quarterly only, always tied to completed goals, and not available to every position), education and training (budget for specific ways to grow and improve in the position), and special considerations (remote work, late starts, early dismissals, or any other factors to consider before a job is accepted). Encourage the candidate to give you a plan that addresses each of these elements and is designed for you to accept without further negotiation.

You'll be pleasantly surprised by the results. When we give our People the flexibility to assign monetary value on their own scale, they build a position that rewards them for what they intend to do well. The process also eliminates any ill feeling about being unfairly compensated because all of the accountability for the offer lies with the candidate. Since adopting this methodology, my candidates routinely surprise me by asking for less wage and more special considerations, often valuing those considerations higher than I would have.

In other words, I pay less for a team member who is more engaged.

Once your candidate returns with an offer, consider it and make the right decision for the business. You are under no obligation to accept their offer, especially if its wide of the mark. You may issue counteroffers, negotiate specific items, or accept some while rejecting others. In finalizing the compensation plan, make sure that you tender a position description and a compensation plan that fully details your expectations. When the two parties have shaken hands on a deal, move forward to the final phase. Because of the filtering you have done up until this point, about 90 percent of your candidates should move on to the Commitment stage. The remaining 10 percent will mostly be those who simply cannot grasp the point of writing an acceptable compensation plan.

COMMITMENT

Finally, your hard work has paid off and you are ready to offer your candidate the position. In the final phase of the interview process, it's time to review with the candidate exactly what commitments are being made on both sides of the deal. This discussion is a two-way street. It involves reviewing the expectations that you and your new team member are setting for each other.

Your commitments to a new team member range from fair

compensation paid in full and on time, to a workplace free of harassment and rewarding of merit, to ongoing training and effective management of results. On the other side, a candidate should commit to produce the highest level of work possible at all times, to engage in the company Culture, to show up on time and prepared, and to be a positive contributor.

Because my business is openly family-oriented, I typically ask candidates to bring a family member to this final meeting. Usually this is a spouse, though I have had candidates bring parents and once even a grandparent! I don't hold it against candidates if they opt not to do so, but I want to make the commitment on behalf of my organization to the People who potentially influence a candidate's conduct that we do all we can for them.

This approach is nontraditional, but it has helped us address obstacles that create problems outside of the workplace. For example, for our commission-only positions, the "lumpy" nature of income, especially for a new hire, can create stress and conflict for families. Having that discussion ahead of time with both the candidate and someone close to her helps puts everyone at ease.

For me, the candor of this approach is part of the secret to keeping employees. When you hire an employee, you are not just bringing the individual into the business. You are indirectly bringing their loved ones on the journey as well, even if they are not personally stepping into the office each day.

Once we have exchanged our commitments to each other, I present the final legal documentation—the job offer, position description, and employment contract—and we shake hands. When we shake hands, I immediately pull out one hundred business cards with their name on it. It's a little touch that demonstrates how much I wanted them on board. I will tell them that the interview process we run keeps us circumspect, but we are very excited about them joining the firm. Just as we appealed to the "I Am" dimension with early praise in the capabilities section, the simple act of handing over business cards sows the seeds for future success.

I believe that CEOs reading this book will have little issue adopting the recommendations I have made. I also recognize that the approach I am advocating may be radically different from what you have done previously. That's precisely the point. Recall how much effort you have already put into your Culture and your values. The commitment stage is your opportunity to live those values and demonstrate them to every employee joining your company.

REAFFIRMING THE PROCESS

Almost every CEO I have met has heard the expression, "Be slow to hire and quick to fire." The data and my experience tell me that most chief executives do the exact opposite. The process we have followed in this chapter is the epitome of hiring slow, though you can condense the process to make a quicker hire when necessary.

The hidden benefit of the 4Cs approach is that it creates discipline. If you know your process is intensive, you will make smarter decisions about when to look for new candidates, and you will experience fewer of those emergency-hire scenarios because your employees will stay longer. In my industry, the average retention rate for an employee is twenty-two months. My company keeps employees for an average of sixteen-plus years. By adopting the philosophy I have outlined, my coaching clients have achieved similar results.

TALENT RETENTION

"*Hiring people is an art, not a science, and résumés can't tell you whether someone will fit into a company's culture.*"

—HOWARD SCHULTZ

The human brain is the most complex system in the universe. It is estimated that the brain consists of more than 100 billion neurons. Tiny junctions called *synapses* link each of these neurons to approximately 10,000 others, resulting in over 100 trillion connections. If the neurons of a human brain were laid end to end, they would circumvent the globe twice over.

Neurons are the building blocks of the nervous system. They transmit sensory information to and from the brain and throughout the body. All of our perceptions, thoughts, knowledge, ideas, emotions, and behaviors result from combinations of electrical and chemical signals passing back and forth among our neurons. For all of this to function smoothly, the human brain needs a constant flow of oxygen.

Although the brain represents just 2 percent of our body weight, it uses about 20 percent of the body's oxygen supply. Without an adequate supply of oxygen, the brain is unable to perform its basic functions, the most important of which is to metabolize sugar and fat into the energy our bodies need to survive. A brain deprived of oxygen for as little as four minutes will fall into a state called hypoxia and begin to die.

Your company is a complex system similar to the human brain. While the brain is comprised of neurons, your company is comprised of People, each interacting with one another on a daily basis. The quality of these interactions determines the quality of your business. Just like a brain, a company need a constant supply of energy to run efficiently and produce the results necessary for survival.

For the brain, that energy comes from the body's intake of oxygen. And for your company? The answer is more complex. People work for two reasons. One is the paycheck, of course, but there are a lot of jobs out there that come with a paycheck. In my experience, People are looking for more than just a paycheck.

Naturally, People expect to be paid for the work that they do, and they should be paid fairly and on time. As Saint

Luke says, "The worker deserves his pay." Pay is a given, and higher pay, while certainly nice, doesn't automatically result in higher levels of happiness, or fulfillment, or satisfaction. In fact, a Princeton study by Daniel Kahneman and Angus Deaton found that making more than $75,000 per year only marginally improves day-to-day happiness.[8] Once your salary has crossed that threshold, your emotional well-being and the pleasure you get from daily experiences don't really get any better.

This is why higher wages don't automatically cause employees to perform at higher levels of work. In fact, it sometimes has the opposite effect, as the complicated interplay of psychological forces drives performance down in the face of what seems like unearned income. In a nutshell, commitment, work ethic, motivation, and job satisfaction are not based on earnings. They are intangibles that come from a sense of purpose and a Culture of appreciation. People want meaningful, fair-paying work at companies that acknowledge their contributions and give them the freedom to be really good at their jobs.

Treat your employees with trust and integrity, and they will do extraordinary things. Deny them that trust, and they will leave. When that happens, your company will fall into a state of corporate hypoxia and slowly begin to die.

---

8   Boushey and Glynn, "Replacing Employees."

IN SEARCH OF THE HOLY GRAIL

Improving employee retention is a corporate holy grail. Nearly every CEO I have ever interacted with recognizes the constant drain on momentum that a high turnover rate causes. The loss of momentum also engenders frustration by forcing leaders to compensate for empty seats at the table, a frustration that everyone in the company can feel. We recognize that hiring and training new employees is costly, and each resignation letter potentially represents a substantial loss in revenue.

All of the work you have done thus far—from building your company Culture up through the talent acquisition process—has been directed toward improving your talent retention. When you craft and nurture a healthy environment and place the right People in it, you naturally curb the most common drivers of employee churn. Recruiting the best People on the planet to your company doesn't matter if they aren't staying with you for the long-term.

Once you've put your Culture in place and refined your talent acquisition process, you can begin to further affect the trajectory of your People in how you manage and lead them throughout their time with your company. Of course, some level of employee churn is inevitable. Even if your Culture is nearly perfect, external circumstances can motivate great employees to pursue opportunities elsewhere. You can, however, dramatically cut that churn to the point that you have a company at which People want to stay.

The first phase of effective retention is for the CEO to find self-control in all employee-related situations, good and bad. From there, the CEO enters the second phase: becoming an absolute praise machine. To implement these processes in your business, we need to build them from a place of love.

THE POWER OF LOVE IN THE WORKPLACE

"Love?! You can't say that word at work!" In the context of business, I understand that the idea of love may feel awkward or uncomfortable. After we explore the idea, you may discover that you prefer a different way of framing the practices I describe in this chapter. But for me, love is the most direct and most apt way to encompass the most effective behaviors a CEO can adopt for both leadership and employee retention.

Today, the word *love* has been reduced to its romantic connotations. Yet the etymology of the word dates back to ancient times when *love* was also used to signify empathy for others. The ancient Greeks had different words for different forms of love. For them, the word *philia* represented the strong bond between People who share common values, interests, or activities—"friendship," if you will. They also used the word *storge* to define the affinity among People who relate to one another because of similar beliefs and practices—familial love, for example. *Eros* was the word used by the Greeks to talk about sensations of physical love—lust. Finally, *agape* was love that the Greeks recognized between God and man, or between man and mankind.

My own concept of the power of love in the workplace is borrowed from Joel Manby, the former CEO of SeaWorld Parks and the author of *Love Works: Seven Timeless Principles for Effective Leaders*. I do not use his entire system, but I find the theme poignant enough that I want to give him credit.

Manby argues that we should be okay with using the word "love" at work and that we ought to treat our People with love without having an ulterior motive. You will spend one-third of your life with your employees, so you should be able to authentically show them love and respect. From a different perspective, Manby's work is a wonderfully practical primer on emotional intelligence.

As you may have gathered, the heart of my CEO philosophy is whole-person management. I counsel my clients that it is not sufficient to operate solely in any single dimension—"I Think," or "I Feel," or "I Am." If you do not understand how your People think and feel, you are not managing the whole person.

You have to manage the whole person, not just that part of the person with the ability to complete a task, and not just the emotional parts of a person either. Your business needs its employees to be balanced and able to face internal and external challenges with focus and maturity. Helping our People do just that is the task of management, no matter the source of their challenges.

Of course, the facet of management that many leaders overlook is that they must first manage themselves. Your own behavior and your leadership have a direct influence on your team, and many of the common reasons that drive good People to leave can be traced back to the behaviors of company leaders. You set the tone with your choices and your actions. You are the CEO, the ultimate example of how employees should think and act. You have to demonstrate self-control in all situations and live the values you claim to be intrinsic to your company Culture.

HOW A CEO HANDLES FAULT

W. Edwards Deming was one of the leaders of what has come to be known as the Quality Movement. Many in Japan credit Deming as one of the inspirations for the economic miracle that saw Japan rise from the ashes of World War II to become the third-largest economy in the world. A key tenet of Deming's philosophy is the idea that "a bad system will beat a good person every time." It was this belief that caused Deming to enjoin business leaders to "blame the process not the people."

Perhaps the greatest opportunity a CEO has within this

framework is how she handles blame. Finding fault and assigning blame is not good managerial practice because we are supposed to be responsible for results and not necessarily the processes that lead up to them. We need to move beyond blame and work on the whole person to produce the results necessary to move the company forward.

If you are naturally critical, or even just outright passionate about your company's mission, the temptation to react harshly when something goes wrong can be difficult to overcome. For example, we once had to fire a vendor because of a host of performance problems. Our companies were not a great fit for each other and we parted ways. During the transition, a member of my team sent a particularly harsh email detailing everything he hated about working with the vendor. There was no point to the email other than emotional venting. It did nothing to advance our cause and represented our firm badly. While his allegations may have been accurate, the handling of the situation was not aligned with our values and our Culture. In addressing it with him, I thanked him for his commitment to holding our vendors to high standards, but counseled him that in the future we should be far more mindful of how fault and blame reflect on our company. I told the agent, "You are way better than the content of this email."

I gave the correction gently and respectfully. This is a guy I love. He made a mistake, but he did not need to be berated for it. The following day, he sent me a kind email, expressed that he was tired and caught off guard by the situation. He admitted that he mishandled the situation and thanked me for helping him regain his sight of the bigger picture.

If you look to humble employees when they make mistakes, you handicap their ability to do better work in the future. Treat each mistake as an opportunity for growth.

A CEO can easily bash an employee for a mistake, but that does not move the person or the business in a positive direction. Yes, there may come a time when you have to remove a person for repeated mistakes, but I would argue that these situations are more often rooted in a Cultural or talent acquisition misstep. If we investigate who is truly to blame in this context, we will often discover it is the CEO.

BECOMING A PRAISE MACHINE

The thirteenth-century poet Rumi once wrote that, "There is a field past the place of fault and blame. I will meet you there." Applying this wisdom in good situations means that we should not revel in our own success too much. You should always look for what you could have done better and for opportunities to praise others instead of taking the credit for yourself.

A CEO has to exercise self-control in both the darkest and

brightest moments. It's important to control your instinct to cast blame in negative situations, and the ability to effectively praise your employees in good times is equally critical. Many CEOs overestimate how often they inject positive feedback into their workplaces and underestimate the impact of their efforts when they do.

The exact practice of praise should be personalized to your business, your Culture, and your People, but your approach to praise will likely have three levels:

1. Individual
2. Collective
3. Familial

Individually, it is incumbent on the CEO and managers to communicate on a frequent basis to let People know that they are appreciated for not only their work but also for who they are. That is an important distinction that mandates your consideration of all three dimensions of a person. Consider this story:

> One day, I was speaking with Tom Purcell, the CEO of Ashford Advisors in Atlanta. We were standing in a hallway at his office, and his new advisors, a group of four, were behind us on their phones scheduling appointments. Our conversation was serious and engrossing, but midway through, he asked me to hang on.

Tom stepped over to a young man, clapped him on the shoulder, and said, "That was great work. If you keep that up, you are going to have a great career." And then Tom came back and continued our conversation, winking to me and saying, "Gotta catch them doing something good!"

The content of Tom's praise was multidimensional. He addressed the caliber of the work he had witnessed and then dove deeper into what it meant for the young advisor's potential. In two sentences, Tom addressed both skill and a deeper layer of aspirational identity. Delivering praise is automatic for Tom. When he sees something praiseworthy, he addresses it without hesitation—even interrupting another conversation so as not to miss the opportunity. At that moment, it became his most important task. It could not be delayed for the sake of our conversation. He instinctively became a praise machine when the time was right.

Our Cultures should encourage frequent and intense praise. Praise for work well done should be featherweight and in keeping with the cultural ritual cadence we've discussed already. A praising CEO finds something to praise People for every day. Receiving praise keeps an employee engaged in his work and conscious that his superiors appreciate his actions.

Praise happens in private and in public. I often take an employee to lunch during the week, pick up the tab and privately offer a sincere thanks for work well done. Believe me, the employee always lets her teammates know that the CEO took her to lunch!

Praise is offered in public too. The tone of any meeting is set by a CEO offering participants sincere praise for good work. Being praised in front of your colleagues makes all of us feel good, but CEOs often wait until highly formal occasions to deliver praise. This is a missed opportunity because when you highlight a praiseworthy action, it shows other team members what the company values. I hope you are starting to see how an act of praise can beget even more praiseworthy behaviors. Praise is motivating and invigorating, and it is a virtually cost-free source of energy that you can incorporate into every aspect of communication in your business, from meetings to email blasts.

At its ultimate level, praise travels beyond the walls of your workplace and into the families of employees. When an employee exceeds expectations, perhaps by staying late or by meeting a critical deadline, you should recognize that in this situation, the employee is not the only one making a sacrifice for the company. Her commitment to the mission took time away from her loved ones, and praise can be a tool for transforming what is typically a stressful, conflict-laden situation into a special moment for the entire family.

Write a note to your employee's spouse to offer sincere gratitude for sharing that time with the company. Recognize the excellent work the employee is doing and make it clear that you see how much she brings to the table. This is a small gesture—a handwritten note takes only a few minutes to write—but it resonates deeply in the hearts and minds of your People.

As you become more deliberate and practiced in praising your People, remember that authenticity is key. If you cannot find a justification for praise, do not fake it. Remain sincere, and remain generous. Eventually, you will find yourself moving beyond statements and using actions, like offering bonus vacation time or a thoughtful gift, as vehicles for praise. With your praise being plainly visible to your People, you will instill in them a desire to praise one another, and your Culture as a whole will begin to support this aspect of your work as CEO.

I am fond of saying to my CEO clients that positivity is the primary product a leader manufactures. Praise is how leaders communicate that positivity to others. Because of the nature of our positions, we can see praiseworthy actions earlier and clearer than others in the organization can. If, for some reason, you cannot find praiseworthy actions in your company, then you have a problem. You either have the wrong team or the wrong heart. Figure out which it is, and fix it.

LETTING GO

No talent acquisition or talent retention process is perfect. The right employee today may experience a life event tomorrow that changes her behavior, or you might mistakenly hire the wrong person, overlooking an aspect of the interview that seems obvious in hindsight. No one gets it perfect every time.

What we have learned thus far are field-proven practices for elevating performance at all levels of a business, and yet, you will still need to fire employees. When that occurs, fire them with love.

That may sound contradictory, but if an employee moved through the entirety of your process and was ultimately not a fit, you cannot ignore that you were at one point moved to work with this person. In part, you bear some of the responsibility for the failure, and it is in everyone's best interest for the employee to be given the freedom to find a workplace where they can thrive. If we choose to hire People in accordance with our values, we should part company with them in the same way.

This is not lip-service or an exercise in mental gymnastics to make you feel better about firing someone. A reasonable person will feel badly about asking an employee to leave even when doing so is justified. My aim is to help you see how firing an employee can be the right decision and how you can do it in such a way that you continue to uphold your values.

Beyond following the legal and ethical requirements for removing an employee—which may include documenting warnings and offering corrective action, depending on your state—you can fire an employee with love by doing the following:

- Prior to taking action, revisit your assessment of the employee's level of work and time horizon. You may discover that they are in fact in the wrong role. It then becomes incumbent on you to find a role in the company that utilizes their strengths, if possible.
- From the moment you first raise your concerns, base all conversations around values. Just as you expect actionable feedback from your People, give your employee constructive and useful feedback that she can use to correct the problems you have identified.
- If that feedback fails after multiple attempts, share your concerns candidly and suggest a path outside of the company that might better suit the employee. Then, support the employee on that path, which may include a severance package, a recommendation for a position at another business (if warranted), or some form of retraining plan.

Not all endings can be happy, but if you act with love, you can turn what is usually a negative experience into something that is, at the very least, productive for the company and for the employee in question.

YOUR VISION FOR TALENT IN YOUR BUSINESS

Throughout our journey, we have worked toward building an environment that is unique to your business and supports the People you bring into it. Your improved understanding of how People work, how you can best go about finding and vetting talent, and what you can do to retain that talent will enable your business to assemble all-star teams at all levels. The amount of work this takes may seem daunting, but the reward is the freedom not to have to micromanage or personally attend to every task for the company to prosper. You will have the right People in place who think and behave in alignment with the company's values while also contributing their own insights into how the business can continue to grow. That is the true power of People that only the CEO can wield.

SECTION IV

—

NUMBERS

LEADING FROM THE NUMBERS

"If you don't know your numbers, you don't know your business."

—MARCUS LEMONIS

The Grandmasters of chess know that the best move on the chessboard is the one that leaves you with the most options. In the game of chess, options are everywhere. Sixty-four squares but only thirty-two pieces, each of which move according to different rules. Making the optimal move—the best of all the available choices—is incredibly difficult. What sets a Grandmaster apart from extraordinarily good chess players is his ability to advance the game—to select from among the full range of options those choices that improve his position on the path to victory.

Throughout history, chess has been considered a strategist's game because victory lies as much in preventing a loss as it does in pushing for a win. Being forced to make a move that damages your playing position is the ultimate humiliation for a chess master. Polish Chess Master Johannes Zukertort famously said, "Chess is the struggle against error." Choosing the worst option is bad enough for a chess player, but being forced to do so by another player—who remains in control of his options—stings.

But how do we know which moves to make and which will advance the game toward your goals? You have to have some way of keeping score, of noting wins and losses, of measuring how well you're doing. Our Numbers—goals expressed in concrete, discrete, comprehensible, and communicable units —are how we accomplish this.

I know that this seems insultingly obvious, but most companies I visit have only the vaguest of goals, expressed only in annual terms. Thoughts like "This year, we should hit $6.5 million in revenue," or "I need to hire three new salespeople before Q3," don't count as goals. They are little more than wishes, and it's easy to understand why.

To illustrate the point, there is a lovely scene in Lewis Carroll's *Alice's Adventures in Wonderland* in which Alice explains to the Cheshire Cat that she is lost:

"Would you tell me, please, which way I ought to go from here?"

"That depends a good deal on where you want to get to," said the Cat.

"I don't much care where—" said Alice.

"Then it doesn't matter which way you go," said the Cat.

Most CEOs do not come from accounting or financial backgrounds, although that is beginning to change. Heidrick & Struggles, the largest executive search firm in the world, recently found that only 30 percent of CEOs at Fortune 500 companies had prior experience in the financial world. For smaller companies, that number is even lower. Accordingly, CEOs often delegate oversight of company finances to someone better versed in the world of Numbers—a CFO, Controller, VP of Finance, or even a bookkeeper—depending on the size of the organization.

In fact, some CEOs argue that Numbers are the sole province of the CFO. As the CEO, you are the primary steward of company resources. Delegation is imperative, but dereliction is anathema. It is critical that you never allow execution on vision and strategy to outpace your financial realities. You must keep enough cash on hand to fund the next move. In business, as in chess, it's a cardinal sin of leadership to leave yourself without any options.

So how does a CEO avoid financial checkmate? By becoming the master of those Numbers which reveal the truth about your business in stark and unbending terms. Math is the language of business. Numbers never lie. Adults deal with reality. Let's get started.

SET THE AGENDA

The person who decides what gets measured is the real person in control of the business. Why was James Madison the first person to arrive in Philadelphia for the Constitutional Convention? Because he wanted to set the agenda for the debates, in which he had little interest in participating. As a result, he is called the "Father of the Constitution" today.

The Numbers we measure, the importance we assign them, the action plans we derive from their interpretation—all of these are examples of the executive function. While you can delegate some of the systems and process surrounding how and when data is gathered and reported, deciding what gets measured is the prerogative of the CEO.

The following might sound familiar: CEOs know that it takes blood, sweat, tears, and treasure to build a successful business. Too often, growth may slow, margins may narrow, and expenses may mount. The company may hit a ceiling, unable to get to the next level with the team and resources available. "What exactly are we striving to achieve?" your People ask themselves silently before embarking on their daily activities, most of which have no connection to end results.

"We need more hard work, more hours, more People. More!" a CEO might say to himself or to his leadership team, secretly hoping that working twice as hard will produce results. We know that success depends on a solid team working together toward common objectives. Yet, it's rare that everyone pulls for the same thing. Why? Because the clarity of your goals is lacking.

Defining your business's key performance indicators (KPIs) is your opportunity to set the agenda. Do you know what Numbers are critical to predicting and confirming success in your business? That's not a trick question. Just as many CEOs lack financial backgrounds, many CEOs measure the wrong KPIs or overlook some KPIs. Every business has a financial Achilles' heel. If not properly monitored and managed, it can cause you to miss important opportunities, or worse, lead to financial ruin.

For restaurants, food and labor costs as a percentage of sales must be actively monitored. Other businesses focus on different metrics. In the retail sector, your key performance indicator may be fixed costs as a percentage of sales on a per-square-foot basis. In the consulting world, gross billable revenues per professional indicates the health of the business. In manufacturing, your illustrative metrics may be inventory turnover or percentage of defective returns. No matter what type of business you are in, you must know your critical Numbers and then build a system to monitor them over time.

Since KPIs are Numbers that focus our attention on those aspects of performance most critical for the success of our business, it is important to note that they can be both financial and nonfinancial. Financial KPIs are typically derived from or directly related to the chart of accounts found in a balance sheet and income statements such as cash on hand, accounts receivable, revenue, and gross profit. Nonfinancial measures are any quantitative measures of business performance not expressed in monetary units. Common examples include measures of client satisfaction, marketing outreach inputs, and other activity measures. Client satisfaction might seem fuzzier than a hard number like net profit, but if you are not tracking client satisfaction, you will not have insight into what makes client retention sag. Furthermore, your People may place less importance on how they handle client concerns if there is no system in place to measure how those concerns impact the trajectory of the business.

As you sketch out the KPIs that represent your business, you will likely see that some indicators—leading KPIs—help you see where you're going, while others help you understand where you are—lagging KPIs. Both are powerful and necessary in driving your business forward. A CEO is the master of both leading and lagging indicators.

Leading indicators reveal how a business is expected to perform in the future—what results are coming our way—and serve as predictive tools. Ideally, they are simple measures of complex activities and provide an early view of likely future performance. They give us the opportunity to intervene before it's too late to correct a negative result.

Lagging indicators are rear-facing, or historical, and reveal the past results of an organization's activities. By their nature, lagging indicators don't provide an opportunity to correct a problem, but they do present a baseline against which leading indicators can be measured. Most businesses only use lagging indicators as KPIs—a dangerous error. That's like driving down the highway and only using your rear-view mirror to stay in your lane.

It is important to be aware of both leading and lagging indicators. Given that sales, profit margins, and cash flow are the lifeblood of any business, CEOs should place particular emphasis on these areas by having easy access to the KPIs that inform them. In setting the agenda and choosing the KPIs that best inform your business, be thoughtful, creative, and wide-ranging. Ask your peers and competitors what key metrics they use in running their businesses. Getting this list correct is critical to success.

Here are some categories that may help you think of worthwhile metrics to track:

- Financial Measurements
- People Measurements
- Sales and Marketing Measurements
- Research and Development Measurements

Each of these categories can be split into subcategories. For example, financial measurements likely include the critical KPIs of profit margin, cash flow, and payment velocity. People measurements might include employee engagement and satisfaction scores, recruiting goals, and even the number of attendees at corporate events. Culture KPIs can focus on ritual engagement, personal growth initiatives completed by your People, and even response rates to culturally themed emails.

Of course, our goal is not to have a flood of Numbers cascading down from every direction. We are after only the key performance indicators. If the KPI for a race car is top speed attained, the idea is that when you see top speed changing—for better or for worse—you can investigate what prompted the change. It may be unnecessary for you to personally track every detail of the vehicle's performance—tire pressure, fuel efficiency, air filter lifecycle, oil change schedules, and so on. Someone should certainly be in charge of those things, but that data may not immediately help you make important decisions.

Once you have drafted and refined your list of KPIs, break them down using a chart as your guide: name the KPI, identify whether it is a leading or lagging indicator, define the formula you use for calculating it, and establish how often it should be evaluated. That final point requires you to strike a delicate balance. You do not want to wait so long to gather your data that you have no opportunity to influence performance, nor do you want to evaluate a KPI so often that you fall victim to every statistical ebb and flow.

Weekly and monthly check-ins are often worthwhile places to start. Quarterly evaluations can be useful, but depending on the business, waiting three months to discover a missed opportunity can mean a significant loss of profit. Choose the reporting cadence that makes the most sense for your company.

SHARE THE AGENDA

A CEO must not only articulate and track the key performance indicators that everyone in the business must pursue at all times, but she must also use those Numbers to instill in her People a sense of ownership. In other words, the Numbers are a springboard for helping your People see the impact of their work and take more proactive roles in moving those Numbers in the right direction. That drives a sense of place and satisfaction within your team, and this is where Numbers and Culture begin to intersect.

As the company finds success with this approach to Numbers, you then have the responsibility to use the results from the combined efforts of you and your People to reinforce the sense of teamwork and collaboration that made those results possible.

Where your People once asked, "Why am I doing this?" they can now begin to understand why it matters to the business. If you frame it in the right way, you can help them to see why it also matters to them as individuals; how reaching that goal is not only good for the business but good for them. I hope that you are beginning to see how Numbers have a far greater potential than many CEOs realize.

Leading from Numbers begins with having worthwhile Numbers. A CEO must articulate the KPIs that everyone in the business should pursue. He must teach his People to track those KPIs down to the level of daily work. He must publish and review results within an appropriate time frame to make meaningful course corrections. His Numbers are his guideposts as he ventures into deeper waters. If he doesn't know where he is, he can't expect his People to know either.

This is happening in most American businesses today. The lack of goal clarity and transparent communication leads to shoddy decision-making, missed opportunities, and malaise among a workforce thirsting for leadership. Any road is the right road when you don't know where you want to end up. Only by establishing leading and lagging KPIs will you to know where you are going and if you are making good progress.

According to a survey by the American Psychological Association, one quarter of employees don't trust their employer. Even worse, the survey finds that only about half believe that their employer is open and upfront with them.[9] Such a lack of trust is often due to a lack of workplace transparency. Transparency is the key to fostering a Culture of trust between CEOs and their teams. People who understand their role in the organization's Culture and goals are more likely to trust their employer and embrace the endgame. Those who are brought into the light know well in advance the challenges the company faces.

This big picture view is important because it will inform how you define, track, and share KPIs. The philosophy behind our use of KPIs provides crucial context to how we use those Numbers to make choices, to lead, and to inspire our People. Our goal is not reductionist. We are not aiming to simplify the whole of our business into cold Numbers. Our intent is more human than this. With the right Numbers and the right approach, we can better understand our People and the customers we serve.

The Entrepreneurs' Organization (EO) is famous for a story

---

9   "2014 Work and Well-Being Survey," American Psychological Association, April 2014,
    http://www.apaexcellence.org/assets/general/2014-work-and-wellbeing-survey-results.pdf.

told by the head of a large mortgage sales organization. In a talk on the importance of Numbers in business, he tells the audience:

> "Everyone has a number...everyone down to the receptionist, who says, 'Three rings bad. Two rings good!'"

While this may capture the essence of the idea, in today's organizations, employees want more than goals and measurements. They want to be informed about the Numbers behind business decisions.

In the days when the clipper ship ruled the seas, a chronometer was the most important piece of navigation equipment in the world. Sailors and mates would be taught how to use a compass and a sextant, but such knowledge was useless without knowing how to read the chronometer, or sea clock, to place that knowledge in context. Only the captain was taught how to read the chronometer, and he wore the winding key around his neck. Letting everyone on the ship know everything was thought to encourage mutiny in times of trouble.

Executives in today's business Culture don't fear mutiny quite so intensely as the sea captains of old, but there is still some reticence of letting People know too much detail behind the Numbers. A middle ground must be staked out, where employer and employee can meet and agree to push the company forward using data as both flashlight and lever. Every CEO knows that leveraging data can mean the difference between success and failure.

Pixable was a digital content creator that relied heavily on social media for its distribution and advertising revenue. In its first year of existence, a team of editors produced saucy content designed to appeal to millennials and tweens. The company was able to demand market average advertising rates even though it suspected that the quality of engagement with its content was far higher than the industry average.

The executive team at Pixable set a goal to increase advertising revenue by an audacious 700 percent in one year without producing any additional content. To accomplish this, the company hired four data scientists to uncover interesting and actionable data trends. Within thirty days, the data team was able to quantify what the executives had suspected: users spent a longer amount of time looking at their articles, shared them more frequently and with more People, and featured them more prominently in their personal social media lives. It was something the company already knew but now had the data to share with advertisers. By building a data warehouse function for these KPIs, and making them available to its entire team, creativity went through the roof.

The marketing team produced a campaign explaining why "Time on Site" was the most important metric for an advertiser to consider. None of their competitors shared that data point with prospective customers. It became an industry-standard metric.

The sales team took the data and customized case studies to specific industry verticals. It used the data to design a new pricing structure whereby advertisers wouldn't pay for advertising that didn't reach its intended audiences at the proper thresholds. By removing the risk of low-performance, Pixable was able to charge a premium for proven performance.

Using data collected by the sales team, the content team then was able to develop a content strategy that only produced articles in categories of interest to advertisers, and delivered the viewership metrics that produced the highest revenue. The advertisers were thrilled by the brand engagement. With the right data in hand, they could spend more while feeling confident that the message was reaching the consumer.

In nearly every business I work with, we discover opportunities hidden in the data. The Pixable story is not an anomaly, but it is rare in the sense that few business leaders take the time to fully understand how their business works, and even fewer share unfettered access to that knowledge with their teams. If you better understand the data of your business, what might you uncover?

OWNERSHIP
THINKING

"The only happy people I know are the ones who are working well at something they consider important."

—ABRAHAM MASLOW

Andrew Carnegie repeatedly referred to Charles M. Schwab as the most effective executive ever born. Carnegie made him President of Carnegie Steel at the age of thirty-five. During his tenure, Schwab once gave a speech on the future of the steel industry to an audience that included J.P. Morgan. The speech convinced Morgan to form U.S. Steel, a combination of the country's largest steel manufacturers into the largest company in the world. Morgan called Schwab's presentation the "world's first billion-dollar speech."

After several years at the helm of U.S. Steel, Schwab left

to take over Bethlehem Steel and built it into the world's most efficient and innovative manufacturing organization. By size, it was second only to U.S. Steel, and it led the market in developing new technologies like the H-beam, which enabled the construction of the skyscraper and the WWII Navy. Schwab's management skills were ahead of his time. He rejected the idea that data was a luxury to be enjoyed only by managers. Rather, he understood how motivating workers by means of a little scorekeeping could dramatically impact productivity.

During the early 1900s, Schwab wanted to increase the amount of steel his plants produced. None of the traditional methods seemed to work. One evening, as the night shift was filing into the plant in Bethlehem, Pennsylvania, Schwab asked a departing day-shift worker, "How many heats did your shift make today?" "Six," came the reply. Without a word, Schwab took a piece of chalk and wrote a large numeral "6" on the floor in front of the production line and walked away. When the night shift started work, they saw the "6" and asked what it meant. "The boss wrote it there," said a man from the previous shift who was leaving for the day.

The next morning, as Schwab walked through the mill, he heard the night-shift foreman shout, "Chalk it up, boys!" When the crowd thinned, Schwab saw that his "6" had been erased and in its place stood a large "7" written in chalk. Seeing the "7" chalked on the floor, a member of the arriving day shift reportedly said, "They think they can do better than us? We'll show them!" At the end of that shift, the "7" had been replaced by an enormous "10"—a staggering number of heats to come off a line during a single shift. In a twenty-four-hour period, production had increased 66 percent!

There are those who see in this story the value of a little friendly competition, but that reading misses an essential point. The only action Schwab took was to provide relevant data to the men doing the job. The men did the rest.

This story illustrates the potential of your Numbers. Once you have synthesized your metrics into easily referenced key performance indicators, you can use those Numbers to lead and empower your teams. The application may not always be as simple as Schwab's chalkboard moment, but the potential is there, and it exists within every business—yours included.

FOSTERING OWNERSHIP THINKING

Creating transparency in your business helps to eliminate the apathy-breeding question, "What's the point?" As your company grows and requires larger and larger teams to operate, even midlevel managers can start to feel that their contributions go unnoticed. When employees begin to feel this way, their actions shift accordingly. They execute some tasks half-heartedly. Others they ignore completely. The dips in performance may be small and isolated at first, but apathy can be contagious. As it spreads, the small losses accumulate, and the trajectory of the business begins to flatten.

Without the number chalked onto the plant floor, Schwab's employees were just going through the motions. There was no measurement. There was no transparency. And therefore, there was no urgency or accountability. By simply sharing that number, Schwab touched on one of the magical aspects of human nature. When we believe our work matters, we are capable of accomplishing extraordinary things.

What Schwab tapped into is now referred to as "ownership thinking," popularized by the book of the same name by Brad Hams. The philosophy of ownership thinking argues that the majority of the modern workforce feels entitled to a paycheck simply because they show up for work. While the idea of entitlement has taken on a stronger connotation in national and international dialogue, I hope that we can at least agree with Hams's conclusion: "The average workplace does not instill in individuals a sense of accountability or a sense of purpose."

Rather than blame the employees for that reality, we as CEOs have to take responsibility for the Cultures we create and view the problem as an opportunity to foster change in the performance of our People. If we can show them the impact of their work and give them a meaningful experience—a sense that their work has purpose and that being accountable for their actions is empowering—we can create a more profitable business and a mentally healthier work-force. Our use of Numbers can be part of the foundation that motivates employees to think more like owners. Here is an example from my own business:

Two years prior to writing this book, I was reviewing my KPIs, and the leading indicators said that we were entering what could become a soft year. I wanted to get out in front of it as early as possible. If we could, I hoped to find a way for us to reduce expenses without firing anyone. If the year was soft as the KPIs suggested, we could come out the other side with the same talent and the same potential that motivated us to acquire that talent in the first place. If the year was not soft, the business would end up even further ahead because it would be running more efficiently.

I brought the whole team into the room, sat them down, and dropped a stack of index cards on the table. "I need to find a hundred thousand dollars of bottom-line profit in the organization today," I said, "and I can't produce a sale to make it. Where can we cut back on expenses?"

I told the team that nothing was sacred, but we all recognized that our goal was not to jump immediately to laying off People. None of us wanted that to be our first or only solution because we valued working with each other. For the next four hours, the team wrote their ideas on index cards, and then we spent several more hours discussing each suggestion. With the entire team present, we discussed the business as a three-dimensional entity, looking at it from the top, the bottom, and the middle, and then we spun it every which way to see what money we could save.

By the end of the day, we found $200,000 of expenses we could cut. Of that amount, $185,000 of that belonged to the business, and we used the remaining $15,000 as a bonus for those who had participated in the exercise. If you put in an idea, you got a share. If your idea was accepted, you got a double share.

We bounced back from the dip even stronger than before, and our People were direct contributors to that success. That is ownership thinking in action, and it would have never been possible if I had not taken the realities of the Numbers to the team and shared with them what we needed to accomplish—not just as a business, but as a collective group of individuals who believe in the same values and want to continue working together. I could not have done it alone.

The CEO as the island, toiling away at leadership as a solo entity, is an archaic idea. You cannot possibly expect to know everything about your business at all times. Your People are on the front lines of your business. Many will have worthwhile insights to share with you, but you will never hear them unless you create an environment where employees have a sense of ownership and are encouraged to speak up.

I once worked with a manufacturing client who needed to improve his production output by 1 percent. The challenge: he had the right practices in place. He had the right equipment. In his mind, the operation was as lean as it could get.

When we went to the teams working the various lines, we learned that one line was lagging in performance. The "bad" line, it was pointed out, often fell behind the other teams. When we delved deeper into the bad line, talking to the team members as well as the managers, we discovered that the bad line was comprised of People being punished by the managers, sometimes for trivial issues. With the entire line made up of either disgruntled or underperforming employees, it was clear why productivity lagged.

By rebalancing the lines, we almost instantly saw an $110,000 improvement in productivity. When we repeated the process with other lines, asking them what problems they saw, we discovered another opportunity to add six thousand annual production hours with no extra equipment or manpower needed. The problem? The factory was still following an archaic workflow protocol, a cooldown safety procedure from the 1970s that no longer applied to modern machinery. It was plant policy to allow a line to cool down for two hours after each run, even though the new machines didn't need any cool down time at all and could run continuously for eight hours. A CEO would never catch something like that, but the worker who has been on the line for fifteen years will, and he won't tell you unless you ask the right question and motivate him to make the business better.

One of the great challenges of gleaning insights from your People is that even if they feel comfortable being honest with the CEO, they may not recognize what elements of their knowledge are worth sharing. When you first begin to foster ownership thinking in your business, you have to nurture it just as you would any other aspect of your Culture. For ownership thinking to be a baseline expectation of how your employees collaborate within the business, you have to seed and guide that expectation over time. There is no shortcut here. You are building trust, and that requires the CEO as well as the rest of the leadership team to behave like trustworthy People.

Ownership thinking is a strategic planning process. If you ask your People about their impressions of the business in distinct categories and work on those areas most in need of focus, you will move the needle much farther and with more internal support than you've ever thought possible. For our clients, we divide the business into ten discrete areas of function. We then survey the team members by asking them to rate the company's performance in each area on a scale of 1 to 100. We compile that data and present it to the management team as a whole. The task is then to "close the gap" between the perceived rating and the highest achievable rating. Closing the gap warrants strategic actions, which are then scheduled and assigned to specific owners.

I personally publish our strategic action plans and distribute them throughout the company. We hire a graphic designer to turn our goals and actions into visual reminders and post them throughout the office. We make those Numbers and the action plan a regular part of our conversations so that the entire company can understand what we are trying to accomplish.

EMPOWERMENT, NOT ENTITLEMENT

It's unsurprising then that many businesses are now looking for easy ways to increase data transparency. Companies that do so see a huge boost in morale and cultural engagement. One of the most efficient and popular methods is implementing an employee-facing dashboard that displays key metrics and supporting data on the state of a business, without role bias, so that everyone can see what areas are performing well and where improvements are needed. That's important. Data transparency does not have to mean complete, unfettered transparency. The more important consideration is this: what do your People need to know to understand the purpose of their work?

For your firm to reach its goals, your team members need to be on the same page. For this to happen, everyone needs to have access to key organizational metrics to determine what works and what doesn't in real time. This ensures that everyone is informed and enables better, quicker decisions.

Studies show that when your team members feel more informed and involved, they put more effort into their work and deliver better results. As employees begin to understand the organization's target metrics, they are able to generate better ideas, test solutions, and solve issues together throughout their departments and the entire organization. More importantly, data transparency promotes open communication by giving everyone access to the same information. Ultimately, using data transparently helps you improve not only your KPIs and overall performance, but also employee happiness and retention.

This is the modern version of Schwab's chalk on the floor. It is also just the starting point. To ensure full buy-in from your employees, you will also need to provide them with context so they don't just know the Numbers but also understand how they should think about them.

DATA FLASHPOINT

In 2008, I convened my team for a basic economics lesson. Our focus was the difference between revenue and margin because I had been told once too often that if I spent $20,000 on a marketing tool that produced $20,000 in revenue, it would be a break-even proposition. But instead of just telling my team that the math was wrong, I decided to demonstrate why.

We met in the conference room, and I held up a $100 bill and asked the team to estimate how much of the bill would be left after I paid all the expenses required to make the money and pay taxes on it. After brief discussion, the consensus was fifty dollars. I challenged the conclusion by raising an eyebrow, smiling, and encouraged them to try again. After an hour's furious discussion, the proper number came out: twenty-four dollars. We run a net profit margin of 24 percent. Less than a quarter of every dollar is mine to take home and live on.

We worked those dollars pretty hard and considered some things as expenses that an accountant wouldn't grant on a tax return. Many of my team members are very successful in their careers with high incomes and a high net worth. Yet they were no better equipped to answer the margin question than those working in hourly jobs. That's because we as CEOs—and as a nation—don't educate People to think in economic terms. The story is still told in our company about the day when we all had our epiphany, and the learnings from that day continue to permeate team discussions without any prompting from me.

It is quite possible that your team is laboring under similar illusions about some aspect of your business. Communicating your KPIs and what they mean for your success is key to dispelling these illusions. If you don't do it, who will? Neglect this, and the members of your team will probably become crash-course graduates in the School of Bad Assumptions.

MANAGING WHAT COMES NEXT

Gathering Numbers is not enough. We have to lead from the Numbers if we are to truly have an impact. Gathering the data, sharing it, educating around it, and planning what should come next are all preparation for the behaviors that bring about real change. Your People must be engaged with the mission of the business, and you have to recognize that their passion for their work is often informed by your passion and leadership.

The best example I have of this comes from my own life. My father, who took over the business from his father, passed away in 2005. That year, he had set a sales goal of $4 million for the company—a 25 percent increase over the previous year's sales. We had never sold that much in our history. By all measures, it was audacious, but he felt that we could achieve it.

When I took over, I shared three goals with the company:

1. Don't lose an account;
2. Don't lose a person;
3. Reach our $4 million goal.

Though I was determined to do anything possible to reach these goals, I was already behind. I had my dad's shoes to fill, and I had to learn the business and learn how to be a CEO at the same time. I studied the business intently and worked long hours, but the only way we were going to reach the goal was if our People made it happen.

We published our sales Numbers on a weekly basis, and on several occasions throughout that year we set sales records. We opened more cases and produced greater revenue than ever before. Several salespeople sold more than anyone else had in the history of the company. Our People loved my dad, and they were driven to honor his memory. His leadership resonated so strongly that it continued to shape their behavior even after I had taken over.

Yet despite these incredible strides, it looked like we were not going to make it. A week before Thanksgiving, I ran the Numbers and anticipated that we would be $100,000 short. It was disappointing, but I was still thrilled because of what we had accomplished. My People, on the other hand, viewed it as a defeat. And they refused to accept defeat.

An employee in our claims department saw the shortfall I predicted, and she took action. This was an employee. Not a manager. Not a salesperson. An employee. She called her mother, who was an HR Director at a school system with over one thousand employees, a massive potential client for our business. She told her mother the story of my dad. She didn't pitch product. She didn't ask to give a presentation. She just shared her passion. That employee got us in the door, and we blew them away. We won the school system's business, and because of that final injection, we ended the year $200,000 over our goal.

That is what leadership from the Numbers can look like. All of us were moved by our mission and our goal, and the outcome was magical.

RETHINKING
NUMBERS

"Life begins and ends with a number."

—CLARENCE AVANT

If the CEO focuses on the Trinity of Culture, People, and Numbers, the aim is to increase revenue and profits. As you enhance your business and watch your KPIs trend in positive directions, the growth of the company will unlock additional opportunities. To sustain the momentum, you must reinforce the changes that facilitated your success, and use your expanded resources to introduce even more stability and opportunity into the business.

Enhanced revenue and profits are not the endgame, though. They are tools that you can use to improve your business and your quality of life while making an impact on those around you. If we simply treat our profits as something to be taken out of the business as a reward for our hard work, we stunt the potential future growth of the business. The apple tree bears fruit, but some of its seeds need to make it back to the ground.

There are many ways to sow the seeds of profit back into the business. If your business is stable, growing, and producing a good return, it should be your most attractive investment opportunity. There is no other business in the world you know more about or have more control over.

SHARING IN THE HARVEST

In the previous chapter as well as in our discussion of employee compensation and raises, we touched on how we should reward our employees for the value they bring to the business. When I asked my employees to find $100,000 in savings, they were rewarded with bonuses—a share of the success they helped the company achieve. They did excellent work, the company recognized it, and they immediately reaped a share of the benefits.

A reward is a compensation delivered for performance beyond the normal course of an employee's duties. It is always tied to a percentage of the value created by the extra performance. It is not a simple carrot-and-stick bonus structure. Those do not work; employees game bonus structures every time they encounter them, and they rarely achieve anything above the bonus threshold. If bonuses were enough to motivate People to give their best work, commission positions would consistently create phenomenal salespeople and bonus structures would be ubiquitous across every industry.

A financial incentive is powerful, but the spirit in which the incentive is shared is important as well. Yes, we want to motivate our employees to be more productive, but our view of productivity must mean more than simply producing more. We want our employees to actively treat the company as if it were their own, and an ownership mindset is much more than baseline productivity. Ownership thinking means thinking about the business critically and creatively. An employee no longer simply punches a time clock and waits for her paycheck. She begins to look for ways to improve the business, knowing that she will share in whatever upside is realized.

The CEO's goal should be to consistently underscore for employees how vital their contributions are to the overall health of the business and remind them that the whole team shares in the bounty of the harvest. That means you have to think deeply about what it means for an employee to bring value to the business. The employee who points out that you are using an outdated cooldown procedure for your equipment does not himself set a new record in individual output. If you relied solely on basic productivity bonus structures, he would never get to share in the rewards that come from correcting this kind of oversight, and as we've seen would never bring it up.

That leaves the onus on you. As CEO, you need to recognize the value that insights and proactive behaviors bring to the business even if you are not directly tracking a relevant metric. Before you cash out your own share, before you put the capital anywhere else, take a moment to see how you can enrich the lives of the individuals who made your success possible. When you see your harvest grow, your first question should be, "Who contributed to the progress we've made?"

Rewards are key, but spot bonuses are useful too. Rewarding those whose actions have improved the operations of the company but fall outside the normal compensation structures is the unique province of the CEO, and employees always appreciate it. I encourage my clients to set aside a small budget each year called the "Private Purse," where these spot bonuses can be granted to deserving employees. Doing so reinforces the discipline of "catching them doing something right," and lets your team know that your keen eye is always trained on those doing great work.

During the COVID-19 crisis, I exhausted my Private Purse by delivering spot bonuses frequently. When People were stressed and out-of-sorts because of the required work restrictions, I used the fund to creatively say "Thanks" and

"Good work" to my team. To the single mom who was home-schooling her kids, nursing a torn meniscus, and keeping up with her workload, I sent a maid over every two weeks to help out with keeping her house clean for her family. To the young single man going without a commission check as businesses slowed down their purchasing, I sent some hand-cut steaks, twice baked potatoes, and fresh salad to him and his girlfriend with a note encouraging them to hold their chins high because things were going to get better. For the vegan married couple, I had some ramen flown in from a favorite noodle shop in California with hand-pressed tofu to say thanks. All of these actions served a dual purpose: they rewarded team members who were doing great work and needed a pick-me-up, and they underscored how we live our values and share the wealth. The lesson didn't go unnoticed, as each of them shared on our weekly calls how much they enjoyed the bounty of love from the firm.

CASH RESERVES

Cash is the lifeblood of any business. Every decision is, in effect, a corporate finance decision because every decision impacts cash at some level. As CEOs, we are often so focused on the getting and spending of revenue that we neglect to consider the benefits of cash reserves.

During the financial crisis of 2008 and 2009, nearly every business owner across the United States faced dire circumstances. As the economy ground to a halt, the just-in-time revenue that many businesses relied upon to fund their operations during times of prosperity dried up. Hardly anyone was buying anything. Even the most loyal customers stopped buying products and services because they did not have the money to spend.

CEOs all over the country were making difficult decisions. Those businesses that survived often did so largely because of their cash reserves. Nearly everyone tried cost-cutting and layoffs. That helped, but the recession was so deep, and the capital needs so great, that simply trimming expenses was not enough. My own business survived largely because of the large cash reserve we had amassed, which saw us through two years of drastically reduced sales. The experience affected me deeply, and it showed me that one of a CEO's Numbers responsibilities is to have a contingency plan in place if the bottom should fall out.

In the game of chess, there is a word for placing your opponent in such a position that you remove every single option she has except for the move you want her to make. In other words, you decide her moves in advance by creating the circumstances on the board. This state of being is called *zugzwang*.

I never want to have my moves as a CEO decided for me, and I don't want that for you either. The only way to maintain your positional freedom in difficult business circumstances is to have a cash reserve built up for emergencies. If you are able to endure hard times, you will not be forced to choose between laying off half your workforce and going bankrupt.

In practice, cash reserves can intimidate CEOs who believe that capital should be put to use. The cash reserve does not necessarily prevent you from leveraging it, but when I suggest that a business set aside a full year's worth of operating expenses, I often see looks of astonishment. Building up a reserve might be difficult, but having that capital locked away is incredibly freeing. Even under the worst business conditions, no one will ever be able to force your hand. That cash reserve, even if you only touch it in emergencies, is a huge source of freedom and autonomy. Your CFO will never look at you and say, "You have to fire someone if you want to keep the doors open." Instead, you have a cushion to brace for problems and solve them long before the wheels fall off.

When you are not staring down a recession, your cash reserve gives you a springboard for pursuing growth. With capital on hand, you can seize opportunities more quickly, better calculate the potential reward of taking a risk, and negotiate new opportunities. You'll be surprised how eager financial institutions are to deal with companies who don't need their help. The rates, services, and relationship you command improve immensely when you have a high cash reserve.

An example from our own operating history: one of my suppliers was concerned about a liquidity crunch during the financial crisis of 2008. We were equally concerned about their ability to meet their promises to us as markets tightened and cash became scarce. The supplier was able to participate in a US Treasury-backed loan program, but only if it shed certain expenses, including its annual sales convention on a private yacht where cabins rented for $2,500 per night. The company had committed to the convention and had put up $1 million to rent the yacht. Knowing our cash position, the CEO asked if I would take over the obligation for $300,000.

Looking at my own balance sheet, and sensing an opportunity, I called a travel consolidator who agreed to buy the cabins for $400K and split any upside with me. I offered my supplier his asking price, $300,000, and papered the deal. After all was said and done, our company made $350,000 on that transaction. We replenished what we had borrowed from the reserve and then had access to more capital that could be applied to strategic opportunities. Without my cash reserve, none of us would have profited from the opportunity.

This is a perfect example of how a cash reserve allows you to act intentionally rather than reactively. If the cash reserve is in place, you can make educated, well-reasoned business choices. When you take the net from under the tightrope, however, looking beyond the step directly in front of you becomes more difficult.

MONEY IS NOT THE ENDGAME

With your cash reserve established—or growing at a regular clip—what do you do with the funds? Just as we should work to acquire money in an ethical and productive manner, CEOs should also give money away productively and ethically. Corporate social responsibility, as the practice of philanthropy conducted on behalf of a business is often termed, can come in many forms and serve a variety of purposes. Your business can donate outright to charities and causes. You can sponsor events. You can donate time or resources to a charity or start a sabbatical program whereby you continue to pay your People as they volunteer their expertise to a nonprofit.

The creative potential of corporate social responsibility is deep, especially when there is a natural synergy between the cause and the for-profit mission of the business. For example, outdoor brands like Orvis and Patagonia devote extensive resources to environmental causes. Their People are passionate about the outdoors, so supporting a cause in line with that taps into an authentic desire to do good.

Of course, charity done for the wrong reasons ceases to be charity, but when wedded to authentic passion and the proper intent, these kinds of programs can improve business results. Choice-savvy consumers see corporate social responsibility as evidence of a trustworthy brand. When a brand supports a cause that aligns with the customer's beliefs, the choice to buy from that brand becomes deeply personal.

Inside the business, a robust corporate responsibility program can help to imbue the work you do with the sense of meaning that is critical to fully realizing your employees' potential. This way, you not only create a powerful ownership mentality but also provide your employees a direct opportunity to do good in their communities, which only adds to them at their "I Am" dimensions. In fact, if the cause resonates with your People, and your program enables them to make more substantial contributions than they would have been able to do alone, you can support your employees across all three of their personal dimensions.

How you apply this idea to your business should be the result of careful consideration and deep discussions with your team. Again, this is an area where your employees will have insights you might not have into causes that appeal to their hearts. Listen to them, let them lead when they feel called to, and praise the results of their efforts.

One of the out-of-the-box corporate social responsibilities I recommend to clients is to partner with a charitable foundation and allow employees to decide how the business's contributions are applied. I often recommend the use of a Community Foundation to streamline this kind of giving. Community Foundations exist in every state. The foundation charges a management fee—a very small percentage of assets under management—for making the investment management decisions, staying in compliance with tax law, and providing back office services that permit you to function like a much larger foundation. Funds placed in these foundations can also be donor-advised, meaning you have direct input into its activities on your behalf. If you work with a Community Foundation, you can rapidly deploy philanthropic efforts, easily stay within legal compliance, and eliminate the complexity and expense of establishing your own foundation, the overhead of which can ultimately stunt your impact. Some of my clients donate up to 10 percent of their gross revenue to their donor-advised Community Foundation funds each month, and they track that contribution as one of the metrics shared with their teams.

That number might be intimidating, but you can set your own number based on what you can donate with consistency and fidelity. It's very important not to view these dollars as lost profit. Leverage your efforts to do good to also benefit the business. If your philanthropic efforts benefit others while also helping you grow, everyone wins.

First of all, these donations are tax deductible for the business. This is a great way of saving money that would ultimately go to Uncle Sam and have it do the kind of work you choose for yourself. Second of all, this activity can enable a range of supporting benefits. Here's an example from my own business:

As I write this book, my firm is preparing to celebrate its fiftieth anniversary. To celebrate, we are giving away $50,000 to local charities. Instead of one lump donation, we are offering five \$10,000 grants. To alert charities of the opportunity, we are getting newspaper, radio, and social media coverage, and that coverage will be repeated when the grants are awarded. When the money is put to use, our People will know that they played a direct role in helping our community.

The boost to our reputation and morale will mean improved recruiting efforts—after all, we want to work with People who want to do good. It will also generate a swell of positive press that might motivate sales prospects to work with us.

If we were to pursue any one of these benefits through traditional methods such as a public relations campaign or a recruiting drive, I would likely have to spend a great deal of revenue. If we donate the money, every dollar spent can support multiple benefits simultaneously, doing something good for both our People and causes we support.

When your business earns a reputation for these kinds of behaviors, you will attract more inquiries and funding requests. This can become a distraction if you do not have a process in place to manage it. In both our business and in the businesses of our clients, we have found that establishing an internal, employee-run board for evaluating funding requests mitigates this distraction. The employees naturally have budget and gifting guidelines, but having them manage the requests for donations takes work off the CEO's desk while also supporting ownership thinking.

THE HORIZON

By following the best practices that I have outlined in this section—from KPIs through ownership thinking through a new way to consider revenues and profits—you can create a leadership dynamic that regularly unearths new opportunities and growth potential for the business. Leading from the Numbers and doing so with engaging transparency will enable you to identify and seize opportunities other CEOs overlook. When you leverage the resulting revenue strategically, you reinforce the behaviors that brought about those positive results, thereby creating a stronger cycle for capturing even more opportunity.

At a glance, it may appear as though you are sacrificing profit by devoting so much of your revenue to employee incentives and corporate social responsibility. You're not. These expenses are investments, and their returns will make an impact on your business, leading to even more profit in the long run.

CONCLUSION

"Continuous effort—not strength or intelligence—is the key to unlocking our potential."

—WINSTON CHURCHILL

Great leaders have two abilities that set them apart from others. First, they can see the innate, untapped potential inside People, a skill that we call *preception*. Etymologically speaking, preception means to perceive something before it becomes visible. It's the ability to see what others cannot, yet.

Secondly, great leaders have the ability to turn that precepted potential into a gift called evocation. Breaking that word down into its roots, we find *ex + vocare*: to call from within. Evocation is the psychological process of transforming another person's potential into reality by them becoming aware of its existence.

For more than thirty years, Madeline Brownlee was Head of The Arlington Schools, a college preparatory academy outside of Atlanta. She was tough as nails, her demeanor accented by an assortment of bulletproof polyester pantsuits and disarming brooches of butterflies and bees on her shoulders. Complementing those pantsuits was an iron fist inside a velvet glove clutching a stone-hard cudgel. You did not play with Mrs. Brownlee.

When I was in the seventh grade, Mrs. Brownlee was my pre-algebra teacher. She believed mightily in the power of homework and assigned fifty algebra questions each night. "Only by doing can we be knowing," she'd say with a twinkle in her eye, laughing at her wordplay over the groans of the class. Each year, she also assigned a "homework monitor," charged with checking to make sure that each student had completed the homework from the night before. In 1986, she chose me.

Completing your homework meant rewards. Sometimes, kids were excused to go to the student lounge for a snack. Sometimes, they were given a study hall to work on other subjects. If you didn't complete the homework, you were invited to a special "Study Session" on Friday afternoon after school. While the session was tutelary and not disciplinary in nature, the effect was that while everyone else was out for the weekend, you and your delinquent friends were in a classroom learning the quadratic equation or Catalan number systems.

As you can imagine, the position of homework monitor was not a glamorous one. Those kids who had done their homework resented being checked; those that hadn't called me names like "narc," "nerd," and "teacher's pet." At a time in my psychological development when my sole desire was to fit in and be like the rest of the crowd, Mrs. Brownlee had set me apart—and I hated it.

Finally, I had enough. Our school didn't have a football team, so basketball was our sport. One Friday afternoon, the season opener was slated to take place at a school more than an hour away. Carpools were forming, bus assignments were being made, and anyone stuck in Study Session would probably miss the game. That day's homework check revealed that several of us had come up short, including the Center for the JV team, who urged me in a forced whisper to "Be cool, man, don't make me miss the game." When I turned in the list of those who hadn't done the assignment, his name was five slots above my own.

That afternoon, I went to visit Mrs. Brownlee during office hours and said that I wanted her to pick someone else for the job. The social cost was too high, and there was no benefit to me at all. I wanted out. She looked over her glasses at me with that classic teacher expression, and a wave of shame washed over me as I saw the disappointment on her face.

"Do you know why I picked you, Mr. Taylor?" she asked.

"No, Ma'am," I croaked.

"I picked you because you can do the job. You know the difference between right and wrong. Not everyone can. I see it in you."

It was a seminal moment in my life. It was as if I had been struck by lightning. I understood everything she meant. Up until that time, I had little self-awareness. Suddenly, that all changed. Mrs. Brownlee had pulled something from inside me by showing me that I was a person who knew the difference between right and wrong and that I had an obligation to use that gift.

I stood up in a daze and began to leave her office.

"Mr. Taylor?" she called after me.

"Yes, Ma'am," I answered turning to see her holding the Homework Monitor Report.

"You also marked yourself as incomplete," she said.

"Yes, Ma'am, I didn't do the assignment."

"Right and wrong, Mr. Taylor. They matter. See you on Friday."

In the years that followed, Mrs. Brownlee would often pull

me aside with a special assignment. "I want to see your name on the Student Council election signup sheet," or "I want you to organize a fundraiser," or "This is a new student, I want you to take care of him." I never said no to Mrs. Brownlee because I knew that she was planting seeds that would later bear fruit.

Today, after more than thirty years of studying human performance, I understand that Mrs. Brownlee precepted that I had certain gifts, and that she was able to evoke those gifts from within me.

Though I may not have had the opportunity to work with you as directly as Mrs. Brownlee worked with me, my hope is that this book has touched you in a similar manner.

If it has, I would love to learn about your business and how you applied the ideas I have presented. Just as the material here is the product of several years of study with business leaders from around the world, I believe that I have something to learn from you and welcome the opportunity to hear your stories and perhaps share them with other CEOs following this process.

And it is a process. As you progress, your business will grow and change. New challenges will arise as old ones fall away. Each new level of success will present a new level of opportunity. To seize those opportunities, you must continually manage the Trinity of Culture, People, and the Numbers. When you do, greatness lies within your grasp.

ABOUT THE AUTHOR

TREY TAYLOR is the Managing Director of trinity | blue, a consultancy designed to provide executive coaching and strategic planning to C-Suite leaders. His experience derives from fields as diverse as technology, financial services, venture capital, and commercial real estate development. Frequently featured as a keynote speaker, he has addressed attendees at the Human Capital Institute, the Ascend Conference, and many other engagements. You can find out more about Taylor's consulting work at trinity-blue.com.